WE KEEP GOING

-M. D. GIBSON.-

WE KEEP GOING

by

ANTHONY ARMSTRONG

Illustrated by Michael Gibson

COLLINS
14 ST. JAMES'S PLACE LONDON
1946

FOR MONICA

FOREWORD

WHEN FIRST I started intermittently writing the story of Margaret Cottage, my intention was merely to provide a short domestic record for the ultimate information and amusement of our two small children. Then along came a persuasive publisher with talk of a "wider public." The result was *Cottage Into House*, a full-length book. This was the complete story of how two town-dwellers bought a tiny week-end cottage and made a small garden; of the great decision—made possible by a successful play—to buy more land, "build on," and live permanently in the country; of the resultant transformation of our little Unencumbered Fee Simple, Margaret Cottage, into a Highly Encumbered Fee Complicated, Margarets, our present home; and of the gradual planning and making of a bigger garden—and incidentally of a bigger family, for it had by then gone into a third edition.

Well, our domestic record definitely did have a wider public; though after all three small children were not a very big target figure to beat.

Encouraged again by the publisher, the record was brought up to date four years later with *We Like the Country*, the story of an originally town-dwelling family's absorption by the country and country life.

A year later *Village at War* saw the light. The tale of our house and garden and family was carried on through the first year of war.

And there I stopped.

All three books had a fair success: at least nobody actually threw anything, as the ham actor said when asked how his Othello had been received. But, as I say, I stopped. First, because in December, 1940, I went into the R.A.F.,

which meant little time for writing books and anyway neces-
sitated living in London; and secondly, because I had begun
to feel that, fairly successful though the books had been,
there was perhaps a limit to the public's interest in the
doings of one family. After all, the whole thing started for
the benefit of our kids.

But in the last year or
so of the war the R.A.F.
job gave me more time to
myself, and various letters
from readers have dis-
played a, I hope, genuine
anxiety to Know More:
"How do you get on with
running the house and
garden when you're not
there?" and "I do sincerely
hope you will take up
the tale where you left
off and tell us what has
been happening," and, in-
credibly, "*Do* let's have
another book about your
family and garden." I'm
all for that last writer:
she's a complete public in
herself.

So at risk of offending those who do not like personal
records, here's another instalment—yet another of what my
family quite brazenly calls the "Us Books." Living in
London, as I have had to do, means there's not quite so
much about the country: on the other hand, the house and
garden have been going strong—to say nothing of the
family—even though I have been so rarely there and have
had to run them by, as it were, remote control.

CHAPTER ONE

AFTER BEING tucked away in a small West Sussex village for the first year of the war, to have to go up and live in London —even though my R.A.F. job was only office work in the Air Ministry—was a definite adventure. For to be in London in the winter of 1940 and spring of 1941 was most certainly, one felt, to be right in the war. It was only to be compared with those May days earlier on, when our South Downing L.D.V., armed to the teeth with elderly rifles and ten rounds apiece, upon occasion mustered hastily at dead of night to repel potential hordes of Hun parachutists. Why, even blitzed Portsmouth, which I visited one afternoon to get measured for uniform, could be nothing to London. London to me wore a veritable aura of ever-present peril.

It is a strange thing about any war, by the way, that the farther you are from any danger zone, the more dangerous that zone becomes in your imagination. One remembers this so well from the first war. In 1916, for instance, our Division was in the line near Armentières. I was in one of the R.E. Field Companies and we worked in the front trenches every day, or night, on various jobs from building machine-gun posts to revetting, drainage, wiring and even occasional trench raids. Going back after work, however, to our little encampment hidden round the edges of a small field, we felt we were practically evacuating ourselves to a safe area. Nevertheless, it was only about eight hundred yards behind the trenches and we lived there for five months solid.

Yet when occasionally gentlemen from Divisional H.Q., seven or eight miles farther back, visited our camp, they gave us the impression that they thought they had practically gone over the top. They wore steel helmets at every

11

pore and peered round corners and kept asking in what direction the Hun was, or telling each other that they were actually "a bare half-mile from the line." They put the wind completely up us; we began to believe, with them, that we in our little camp were living in constant danger—till we realised that quite possibly their own safe haven of Divisional H.Q. must have seemed equally dangerous to visitors from the Base at Rouen—"Why, it's only a bare nine miles behind the line."

Well, so too did I feel when leaving Midfield Station that drizzling December afternoon—seen off into battle by my wife, Monica, and the two daughters, Toni and Felicity. A sort of "Say good-bye to your father, darlings, he may never come back" atmosphere hung over the parting. I remember I took up my gardening gum-boots, a sweater, and a pair of old flannel trousers to keep handy by the side of my bed; it was my conception of the ideal "bombed-out-at-midnight" costume for the man-about-London.

After all this I was quite surprised to find Waterloo Station a hive of activity—though minus roof-glass and thus very wet—and almost indignant when I reached Hampstead, where I was going to live in my mother's house, to discover not a single pane of glass missing anywhere in the street. On top of this I found that my old mother was still occupying her first-floor bedroom and continuing to occupy it whether a raid was on or not—whereas I had fully imagined that on bad nights she went down to the ground floor at least, if not to the basement. But no, it took more than Goering and his pals to shift her from her bedroom by any means other than a direct hit.

She was, of course, becoming very deaf, which helped, because unless a bomb was near enough to shake the house a little, or the Primrose Hill or Hampstead Heath guns fired directly overhead, she was unaware of the strength of the raid. Her only fear was of being bombed when in her bath, and, since she rarely heard the sirens, I had to keep her posted as to the existence or not of an "alert." One particularly violent evening about ten o'clock, I remember, she did hear something when a bomb burst not far away in Fitzjohn's Avenue. "Ah," she said happily, gathering up her knitting, "there goes the 'all-clear'; I think I'll go and have my bath." On another occasion a fairly near one in the Pond Street or Fleet Road neighbourhood shook the old house to its core —and to my surprise apparently caused the old lady the utmost delight. I couldn't guess what the hell she'd got to be pleased about, till she said, beaming all over: "My hearing seems really to be getting better, my dear boy; do you know, I distinctly heard some quite distant gunfire."

Her bad hearing had other advantages too. She did not hear the wardens shouting rude things about her black-out— or rather lack of it. For, being of a thrifty "make-do" disposition, she had refused so far to buy proper black-out curtains, but had hung elderly spare curtains behind existing ones and used bits of brown paper to fill gaps. What with the real curtains rarely being drawn properly by herself or the cook, and the understudy curtains having holes, and the paper getting torn or coming unstuck, she was the local A.R.P.'s big headache. After a bit they gave up complaining at mere chinks, and merely concentrated on complete windows being overlooked while raids were actually in progress.

But after I'd been installed some time and had been involved in several heated arguments late at night with police and others, I bought proper black curtains and overhauled the whole system. The result was, I believe, a protest from local residents who then got lost every night on their way home, deprived as they were of the guiding beams of my mother's well-known black-out, which apparently was one of the after-dark landmarks of that part of Hampstead.

Talking of my mother's reaction to raids, by the way, reminds me, quite irrelevantly, of my wife's mother's famous report to Monica of a raid on Bournemouth where the old lady was staying. She wrote describing where the bombs fell, "one in the centre of those gardens, dear, you used to like so *much*, and another in High Street, and you know that little hotel on the front where old Mrs. Higgins *always* sat *every* morning on the veranda—well, the veranda received a *direct* hit, and Mrs. Higgins would have been *killed outright*, if she hadn't died a year before war broke out."

My mother-in-law came from Ireland.

For the first week or so of my life in Hampstead I continued to have that front-line feeling and religiously laid out my old trousers, sweater, gum-boots and so on by the side of my bed each night in case of a call from a Hun bomb —much as a doctor probably lays out his baby-delivery hand-bag before retiring to rest. Then I realised I was going to too much trouble for comfort of mind, and anyway they were my only gardening rig and more useful at home. So when I next went down to the country I took them back to report for their rightful duty. After all, they were my oldest clothes, and what can be dearer to a man's heart?

It is funny—and just another of those differences between men and women—how new clothes are one of woman's supremest pleasures, while really *old* clothes are what makes a man happy—especially if he is an enthusiastic gardener.

Apart from the delight of wearing clothes that you can't spoil and which aren't therefore constantly on your mind and so distracting attention from whatever messily masculine job you are doing, you can't garden properly in anything *but* old clothes. Gardening means pushing about in shrubberies while pruning, going down on your knees while planting out, digging, forking manure, crawling under greenhouse staging for the leaf-mould, getting tangled up like Laocoon with dead rambler tentacles and so forth. You can't do that in anything but the most antique suitings. Above all, gardening means things in pockets— bass, nails, twine, labels, pencils, knives, even sécateurs, and nothing but the oldest jacket can cope with that. I fully

realise that the pocket linings may
also be too old to hold these things,
but in my experience it means you can
carry more of them—all down inside
the coat itself—though you have to
dive deeper of course.

Women can't really understand this
—well, wives rather, for have not a
pair of ancient gardening boots be-
longing to Miss Jekyll of Minstead
fame actually sat for their portrait
in their own right—and got into the
Academy too? Wives as a rule want
their husbands to be well dressed at all
times—largely because they themselves like to be well dressed at all
times (and their idea of being well
dressed is a pretty uncompromising
one—"My dear, I *can't* be seen out in
these rags," means probably a button
loose or something). As a result, a
state of intermittent subterranean
warfare generally exists in any country home over what the
man wants to wear. And if he has any *really* old clothes he'll
do well to keep them under lock and key.

I remember once a friend telling me about a time when
all the wives of his village ganged up on the men. It seems
that every year the village held a sort of "do"—jumble sale,
stalls, bowling for a pig and whatnot—in aid of local
charity. It was known to the "quality" as a "Feyte" and to
the villagers as "The Feet." To this jamboree protesting
husbands were annually dragged in order to help make it a
success. Why this should be I don't know, except that
possibly woman, the holder of the housekeeping money, has
an inborn objection to parting with good cash for, say, a
set of hand-embroidered egg-cosies even for the benefit of

the local Cottage Hospital; whereas a man, held firmly in
tow by his wife, will even fall for a pound of chocolates
bought that morning at the village shop for three and six,
divided between two pink boxes and sold at five shillings
per box. (Before the war, of course!) Moreover, it is a
curious fact, but with plenty of men at a Feet you can always
raffle a series of ten-bob cakes for anything over a couple
of quid each, provided you get a bunch of attractive girls
to sell the tickets. This is more than a curious fact, it is a
Natural Law.

Well, one year the men of this particular village went on
strike by arranging some sort of tournament at a neighbouring golf club on the same day as The Feet. (The Feet was
nearly postponed when the news got out; but the Vicar's
wife said it would be a sign of weakness.)

Next year, however, the wives got even. Not only did
they wipe out the natural deficit (due to male absence) of
the previous year, but they made a record profit. It was done
by means of the jumble stall. A few days before The Feet
every single man missed that favourite old coat, or grey
flannel gardening trousers, or treasured sweater. Wives
apologised for the error, or justified themselves, or pleaded
charming ignorance; but the fact remained: the things
had gone to the jumble. And on one thing all wives were
united: they could not in common decency be demanded
back. No man could be so hard-hearted as to snatch from
the tentative grasp of a Cottage Hospital an old, a very old,
coat. There was only one way out: go to The Feet and buy
back the treasures.

Husbands fumed, but the logic was unanswerable. Wives
were accused of tricks and treachery and answered sweetly
that husbands of course needn't go to The Feet; they were
perfectly free to go up to one of those golf club parties if
they wished. In which case some of the poorer villagers
would no doubt at once snap up the garments, if they were
really as valuable as husbands made out. The most that

wives could do to rectify matters would be to arrange with the stall-holders to put such a high price upon the garments in question no villager could afford it.

They did. Moreover, their ideas of a high price were extraordinary. They said afterwards they wanted to be sure the articles *were* out of reach of villagers.

Husbands with tears in their eyes and catches in their voices swarmed round the jumble stall. Favourite coats were at least three or four quid; treasured sweaters a guinea and a half. Husbands came away crooning to themselves over parcels, and the Cottage Hospital started up four more beds.

But the following year, my friend told me, every husband slept in his gardening clothes for at least a week before The Feet.

While on the subject of village Feets, I am reminded of some lovely old posters advertising local village sports of about a hundred and thirty years ago. They were hung as curios in the bar of The Feathers, the inn at Holt, Norfolk, where I occasionally stayed when visiting my son, Jomfrey, at Gresham's School half-term. One was dated July 6th, 1814, and advertised "FRAMLYNHAM FESTIVAL. RUSTIC SPORTS." I can't remember all the items, but the following one took my fancy and I copied it down. It was: "A CHEMISE RACE FOR SIX LASSES. *The winner of Two Heats to receive a Chemise elegantly decorated with True Blue Ribands. The Second winner of two heats to receive a pair of Stockings and Garters with the Trafalgar Motto*—ENGLAND EXPECTS EVERY MAN TO DO HIS DUTY. *Each fair lass to be supplied with two yards of Riband to decorate her hair.*"

The other poster, of about the same date, announced: "VARIETY RURAL SPORTS AT WANGFORD." Amongst other attractions it offered: "DIPPING IN FLOUR FOR MONEY. WATER FOR ORANGES. *The boys not to wear Caps and their mouths not to exceed Six Inches.*"

There was also a "GRINNING MATCH OR WHICH IS

THE UGLIEST MUG." One would have thought that explicit enough, but the poster, obviously composed by the local literary wag, amplified it thus: " *The match will be contested for by men of all ages, short or tall, little or big, fat or lean, young or old, grave or gay, and must be performed according to the usual custom on these occasions, exhibiting the various contortions of the human face by grinning through a horse-collar. The winner to receive 2s., and the other competitors to have One Gallon of regular clamber-down, knock-me-down, sew-me-up, do-me-brown, ask-me-how, come-it-strong, out-and-out Wangford Ale.*"

Apparently beer in those days must have been something less than 3d. a pint, if the first prize of two bob was to be well and truly striven for, which "makes yer think, don't it?" At present-day prices the prize would have to be round about 12s. 6d. if they wanted me to concentrate on *winning* the competition rather than on being an "also-ran."

Another pleasant item in the same Rural Sports was "A RACE FOR FEMALES FOR A HANDSOME GOWN-PIECE." Knowing what can happen at bargain sales, I imagine that this must have been good fun, but obviously the promoters didn't want to have any trouble on their hands because they hastily went on: " *Married Ladies will be allowed to contest for this prize by having their Husband's consent.*" A further nice touch was given by the added and somewhat unexpected admonition: " *Single Ladies to wear Drawers.*"

Evidently they were a bit prudish in those days! The spoil sports!

But let's stop digressing and get on with the good work.

CHAPTER TWO

As I mentioned earlier my job was only an Air Ministry
one, and once I had got into my stride, I settled down into
a sort of routine for my visits to Margarets. The
"Chairborne" troops working in the Air Ministry were
allowed one "rest day" a week, generally Sunday, but as
far as my getting home was concerned, the day of rest
would have been mostly a day of travel. By working straight
through, however, I could put two week's rations together
and get a couple of days at home per fortnight. I could not
put three weeks' rations together: for some Service reason
it then became "leave." And not *two* rest days plus *one*
day's leave either, but *three* days' leave against your annual
allowance—and no credit for rest-days.

I pretty soon discovered, too, that a mere couple of days
a fortnight was not very much for a keen gardener. In the
old days, except for the occasional day in town, or walk,
or picnic with the kids, I used to work in the garden every
afternoon. At least *I* used to call it work—what my Mr.
Friar, the gardener, called it I don't know, for he did nearly
all the heavy digging in the vegetable garden. As I used to
point out to him, he was, after years of experience, so much
better at it than I was. And after all I did once justify
myself, or rather showed the world what I could do, by
personally and unaided digging up the site of the tennis
court in the first autumn of the war in order to Grow More
Food. (It was known locally as the "Armstrong War
Effort.") So as a general rule I looked after the flower-
garden side of the business (the "gay ground" as Sussex
dialect has it) with all the sowing, transplanting, weeding,
potting-up cuttings, and so forth, as well as more weeding,
nursing the flowering shrubs and roses and the pruning of
both of these, not forgetting weeding again, while Friar,

under my vague supervision as proprietor of the business, ran the vegetables, at which of course he was an expert.

But two days a fortnight—especially when I had suddenly to turn into the man of the house and father of a family once more, with all that that implied in the way of bills, odd jobs (from repairing door-locks to helping wash up and fill the stoves), children, correspondence, and even writing occasional articles or stories, to say nothing of the general feeling of being home on leave—well, just about the time I was ready to tackle the garden, it was time to go back. However, the invaluable Friar always kept things going, particularly those all-important (in war-time) vegetables, while Monica did as much flower-gardening as she could in the masses of leisure hours she had between housekeeping, cooking, sweeping, dusting, bed-making, jam-making, mending for three children, Red Cross and Women's Institute.

When I got home, therefore, my normal procedure was at the first opportunity to inspect—generally with Monica— my beloved garden in order to see how it was looking and what had come out—or died—in my absence. Then I would mark down several jobs that I thought had to be done—ones of course which I particularly liked doing—and would devote my two afternoons to them, if nothing else cropped up.

Naturally such jobs had to do with the flower side of the Estate. I had got rather vegetable-minded during the first year of war, when it seemed almost unpatriotic to have flowers in one's garden at all. But now I was in uniform I felt that unadulterated flower-gardening might be allowed as a relaxation to one of our brave Chairborne Troops fresh from the battlefields of the Kingsway Air Ministry.

I well remember the principal job I set myself on my first two days at home after Going Off to the Wars on the London front. It was to take the chrysanthemum cuttings. Indeed I had been all set to do it when the trumpet sounded for me and I had to rally to the dear old flag.

We had, the year before, been given by the friendly head-gardener of a large house near-by, a number of indoor chrysanthemums. We stood the pots in bowls on the floor in the hall facing the doorway, and they made a grand show of colour in November and early December. In case it's of interest to readers, here's a list of the varieties we had. You must, of course, remember they were not our choice—beggars can't be choosers—nor were they necessarily the best varieties; they were just what our friend decided to give us. But we found them extremely good, and quite a representative collection, too.

There were four very nice Single Decoratives: "Molly Godfrey," a pleasant pink; "Susan," a rich rose colour, a sport from "Molly Godfrey"—probably only modest Molly blushing after overhearing a doubtful joke; "Golden Seal," a very deep shade of yellow and very highly spoken of by the experts; and "Democrat," a beautiful bronze with a yellow centre, and very highly spoken of by me. Then we had an Incurved called "*Emblême Poitevene*," orange-yellow; and three Decoratives: "Balcombe Beauty" and "Algores Yellow," both golden yellow; and "*Blanche Poitevene*," which was white and served to show up the other colours when in the house. Finally there was a chrysanthemum called "*Wizard*," which was in colour a wizard bronze, as the Air Force would say. This we were told by the donor we would not find in any catalogue, as it came from some special chrysanthemums grown at Belvoir Castle, where he had been gardener before coming to East Downing and where apparently several cuttings "fell off" as he went past. We were rather impressed with its lineage, and the other varieties touched their petals to it when they passed, and deferred to it like anything.

Anyway the whole lot of them made such a good show the first year that I decided to repeat the performance next year, and was told that I should "take cuttings in the usual manner," as the stools were apt to grow old and pot-bound and flower rather poorly. I inquired into the taking-cuttings business and ever since then we have done it regularly, though some of the original varieties have died.

Well, this is what we do. (It may or may not be the proper experts' way: it is only my recollection of what the experts told me and has probably suffered a sea change.) When the plants finish flowering—early December or before —we cut them down to about five inches of stem and put them out in the greenhouse. Here scanty but regular watering will, round about January, bring up shoots from the old stool and these—although they don't know it yet—are to be groomed for stardom to make a smash hit on the Margarets' hall stage next winter.

There is one important thing to look out for in taking these cuttings, so I was told, and that is to be sure you get the *right* ones. However suitable and attractive a possible shoot may look to you, find out just where it is shooting *from*.

To do this, scrape away a little of the earth and if you find it is just coming straight from the old stem, refuse to play. These are actually only young flowering *branches*, breaking out because you've cut the plant down. Probably you'll even see small buds at the end: even if you don't, they're still there in embryo. Mind you, I don't say you can't strike them: you'll be able to all right; but *don't*; they're considered wrong!

The shoots you want are the young plants, as opposed to branches. They come more or less from the stool itself, "basal shoots" they're called, and they'll be through the earth very often quite a distance away from the old stem. They are the real chips of the old block.

Cut them cleanly across, well below the surface and just under a joint, take off a few leaves at the bottom, and strike them in a deep box of fine loam and leaf-mould mixed evenly, moistly, and lightened with sand. Press it well down round the cuttings and put a sheet of glass, if you like, over the box to help start them off, but remove it when they begin to stand up and face the world on their own. In about a month they'll be ready to be potted and you can also start pinching them out to achieve bushiness.

Then keep on pinching them out—and re-potting with bigger pots—right up to the end of June if you wish, though by April they should have been moved outside. Soot-water and bone-meal are good things to use to bring them on and don't forget a stick to tie them to. And then at the end of September in they come, and all you have to do is to listen to your wife saying, "My dear, how marvellous!" That is, if she's the right sort of wife.

One of the non-flower-garden jobs, however, which I insisted on doing myself during an early two-days' leave, or "forty-eight," was to spray the peaches. I had always taken a personal interest in this, chiefly because in August and September I always took a more than personal interest in the peaches themselves.

The idea of spraying is to prevent "leaf-curl." This is a disease to which peach trees apparently are particularly prone. You suddenly find young leaves have developed swollen, bloated red patches, rather like the complexion of a retired colonel who's been too fond of port all his life. Occasionally patches do not turn red but remain green (maybe it's a colonel who prefers *crème-de-menthe*), but there's no mistaking the bloatedness. The affected leaves soon crinkle up and drop off, till, if you have it badly, the trees get practically bare. We have at Margarets three peaches— or rather two peaches: one early ("Peregrine," mid-August[1]) and one a month later ("Violette Hative"); and a nectarine ("Lord Napier")—all fan-trained on the nine-foot-high south-facing wall of the walled garden; and about a couple of years after they'd been planted, the leaf-curl moved in on them in a big way.

I made inquiries as to (*a*) what the trouble was, and (*b*)

---

[1] In 1945, when everything seemed extra early, I had the first peaches on 28th July.

what to do about it, and gathered that it was a sort of fungus
and that what I had to do to prevent it was to spray them
a month ago—before even the blossom, which came before
the leaves, had opened. This wasn't much immediate help.
The only thing I could do at this stage, it seemed, was to
control it by picking off all affected leaves as soon as they
showed up. Ultimately a second crop of new leaves would
appear, but the important thing was not to let any of the
bloated ones hang around on the tree or the ground below:
otherwise the disease, being a fungus parasite, only gets
distributed about the place.[1]

The actual spraying—which is prevention, as against
controlling—should be done shortly before the buds open,
i.e., end of February to early March, not after; and it should

[1]For the same reason you should, of course, *burn* all leaves you pick off,
not merely throw them away on the rubbish heap.

25

be done on two occasions about ten days or so apart, so as to catch what you missed the first time. The stuff to use is "Bordeaux." By this I don't mean you should spray your trees with a bottle of Medoc: you can probably think of a much better use for a bottle of Medoc—and so can I, if it comes to that. Bordeaux is a well-known copper sulphate preparation, which you buy at any suitable shop. A thing to remember about the spraying is that Bordeaux mixture and Burgundy mixture is insoluble in water, so you must keep stirring it up while spraying; otherwise you'll find most of it left in a sludge at the bottom of the pail when you've finished.

Another thing which I have always found well worth while doing to ensure a good crop of peaches, is to take a soft paint-brush one dry morning when the bloom is open and pollinate the flowers by hand—just dipping the brush lightly into the centre of the flowers one after the other. The weather can often be pretty chilly at peach-blossom time and many of the bees and other insects that should be on pollinating duty prefer, wisely, to stay at home and sit by the fire. So muttering "slackers" under your breath, you set about doing the work for them, looking rather like a cross between a portrait painter on a country outing and an oculist performing a series of delicate cornea operations.

When thanks to your labours you have masses of young peachlings nicely set, you may consider they need thinning out, so that instead of a lot of small peaches you get fewer but fatter ones. This is up to you. I personally have so often found that when I carefully pick off, say, three out of a cluster of four, the fourth goes and falls off on its own a moment later.

It's as well to remember, by the way, that young peaches are apt to fall off if they don't get sufficient water, just as they have set. So watch out for droughts at that time. And when you do water, don't sprinkle. Slosh about five gallons round the roots.

In spite, however, of drought, leaf-curl, and the rest, I must say we've always done very well with our peaches at Margarets. (Since writing this I've been out in the garden and picked two perfect "Violette Hative's" each weighing 8½ ounces and measuring over 10½ inches round.) I attribute this largely to pollination by hand in the spring. The only year it wasn't done—because I was not home at all at the right time and Monica considered the bees seemed to have the matter under control—there was quite a noticeable falling off in the fruit. Personally I think it's too much of a risk leaving it to the bees alone, when you consider how marvellous it is to be able to go out before breakfast and nonchalantly pick half-a-dozen peaches for the family— especially when you, while eating them later, reflect that each is worth at least six shillings in a London shop. It puts one on a level with a Roman Emperor tucking into a dish of larks' tongues, or even Cleopatra drinking that famous cocktail with a costly pearl as the basis. ("The heart of a good cocktail is a pearl-of-great-price."—*Advt.*)

With our nectarines we were never quite so lucky. They had a distressing habit of splitting before they were fully ripe and thus were simply a dead snip for the wasps.[1] By the time they were ripe enough for us to eat, the wasps had eaten half of them. If we picked them to ripen them out of harm's way, the split portion started to go bad, and in any case a nectarine doesn't keep long after being gathered. We tried covering them with muslin bags one year, but it was too much of a business and as often as not a wasp got in. Many years we barely got a single nectarine as dessert, but had to stew or make jam of what decay and the wasps had left. But it all goes to prove what fine fruit we grow—for our wasps are most frightfully particular!

[1] The reason for this splitting of nectarines is still rather moot—even, I believe, among experts. It is partly due to too much water when the fruit is swelling which makes the stones crack, but some say that the trouble goes even further back and it is caused by the fertilisation being only half effective.

CHAPTER THREE

IT DID NOT take me long to discover that the new life had suddenly cut me off very much from my children. Being a free-lance writer, and therefore having my office and factory on the premises, I had naturally been accustomed to seeing a good deal of them—though perhaps not so much of Jomfrey, who by then had been at boarding school for over two years. Two days only a fortnight was rather an abrupt transition. And when after a couple of years Toni also went away to school, it meant that I only got them all three together when my visits home occurred in holiday time. On the other hand, remembered from afar and viewed only occasionally at close quarters, they began to seem to me far nicer children than when swarming all over the house.

Monica, however, turned out to be a marvellous correspondent—a fact I'd almost forgotten since we got married. Not only did she pass on to me the better extracts from Jomfrey's letters and, later on, Toni's—for to ask them to write the "weekly letter home" to *two* parents was too much —but she also reported in amusing detail all doings about the house and garden.

There was, for instance, the time when Felicity arrived home in tears from her day school in the next village. It seemed that walking along the road she had found a small and very dead baby rabbit. Only one thing to do with the find, of course; take it home to Tabs, her personal cat, who was at the moment not well and obviously needed an invalid diet.

So the rabbit was wrapped up in a dock leaf, but just as home was reached a tough-looking black tom—evidently lying in wait athwart the trade-routes—leapt out from a hedge, snatched the prize and proceeded to eat it in front of her, warning the impotently tearful owner off all the while by a bloodthirsty growling. As Monica wrote, it was a clear case of hi-jacking.

Another incident in Felicity's young life, which enlivened my Air Ministerial existence considerably, was the writing, at the age of six, of her first anonymous letter. Come to think of it, it's a bit of an incident in anyone's life at any age. Apparently she announced to Monica one day that there was a child named Alice whom they all disliked. "So we wrote her a letter and put it in her locker where she'd find it and not know who sent it." Pressing for details Monica discovered that Felicity herself was the chosen poison-pen-girl and that the actual wording of the anonymous letter was this: "Dear Alice: We think you are a beast. We, Robert and Judith and Betty and Ann and Teddie and me, wish you would go away." Not overwhelmingly anonymous, and the best part of it was that it ended in the only manner known to letter-writers of six years old—"With love from Felicity."

Toni, too, frequently came into the report sheet in a big way, but her efforts were of quite a different character; causing generally the utmost annoyance and inconvenience to all. Not deliberately: it was apparently a sort of instinct. Her triumph, I was once told in a frantic letter from Monica, was when, due to go back to school early next morning and with all her luggage sent already in advance, she went off just before tea to say good-bye to a young friend who lived at a farm just down the village. As she was wearing her school uniform, with a brand-new coat and all, ready for the morrow, she had strict orders to (i) go, (ii) say good-bye and (iii) come straight back, without stopping to play any sort of games whatever.

The fact that her friend was just fetching a couple of ponies in from the field was too much for her. Within five minutes they were careering bare-back in mad chase round the field . . .

She turned up half-an-hour late for tea and timidly

announced through the dining-room window that she'd had a "sort of accident." Monica, annoyed, asked what had happened. Toni had, it seemed, while saying good-bye very correctly, sort of found herself on horseback: not a game exactly, just to see whether she *could* ride bareback in her school clothes. Then the other horse, as it were, began to trot, and then sort of gallop, and of course her horse had to follow it, and it couldn't *quite* catch it up. . . .

After a bit, it seemed, Toni's horse came abruptly up against what she described as a sort of manure-heap. The horse stopped: Toni, however, went on. . . .

It wasn't till Monica bade her come into the house at once so that she might know the worst, that she realised that Toni's rigmarole of understatement had concluded with the best example of all. The "sort of manure heap" was, in point of fact, a good old-fashioned country cess-pit. And Toni had to leave at dawn the next day in her school clothes. . . .

Monica concluded this particular letter with, "What would *you* have done, chum?"

Occasionally, of course, in the later years I was honoured by receiving letters direct from either Toni or Jomfrey at school, but they were pretty formal affairs, containing polite remarks like: "I hope you are having weather," or better still, "the weather here is very intermittent," or an announcement from Toni that "the matron said yesterday I was contissipated." In one communication Jomfrey, whose spelling also was somewhat original, took a plunge into world affairs. During the African campaign he wrote: "I hope we soon get all the top of Africa and assolt Cecily." After feverishly checking over in my mind his circle of feminine acquaintances, light dawned. I could only toy with the idea of writing back, "make certain she's over the age of conquest."

But in general the letters I received from the children personally contained some direct request for goods or services: Monica was the family clearing-house for news—such as the surprising information from Jomfrey once that in his dormitory the prefect's method of arousing enthusiasm in the boring business of undressing and going to bed was to organise games of "strip *vingt-et-un!*"

Naturally the children did not come up to London much for fear of the bombing, but Felicity clamoured so importunately to see this wonderful place to which she had never been, that Monica once organised a brief day excursion for her benefit. After all, to have attained seven years and yet have spent one's whole life in the country, rather labels one as the stay-at-home type.

So up to town Monica and Felicity went. I believe the sortie as planned was seeing Buckingham Palace, feeding the ducks in St. James' Park, lunch (*with* ices and fizzy lemonade *through* a straw) at Lyons, and then a Disney programme.

Actually it didn't work out like that. The myriad railway lines outside Waterloo Station were the first really big thrill —after, of course, the actual railway journey, for Felicity was a child of the motor-car age and had only once before been in a train.[1] Then came the station itself, with the bustle, the engines at close quarters, and the dog collecting money. A comparatively sober little walk led next to Hungerford footbridge and this was considered "tops." For not only did tugs, barges and so on pass right underneath you, foaming up against the tide and current, but trains ran on the very same bridge, shaking the whole place alarmingly, and so close they could almost be touched. And by the time Felicity had also actually crossed a street with trams by the same bridge and descended a marvellous openwork iron staircase, she'd taken on about all she could stand and was demanding to go home again. She'd *had* London. The place was absolutely all it had been cracked up to be, and she was glad to have had the opportunity of seeing it.

[1] A girl in our village of East Downing, only fifty miles from London, who helps Monica with the house work, actually never rode in a train till 1942 when she was 18½.

MICHAEL D. GIBSON.

The other two children naturally were in London more often, on their returns to and from school, and I often met them there, acting in the rôle of dispatcher, meeter, and provider of interim lunch and entertainment.

Encounters with Jomfrey on these occasions during my five years in London ran right through a gamut. In 1941, at twelve years old, entertaining him meant principally ices, and all he wanted to see were (a) Mickey Mouse and (b) a bombing raid on London while he was actually there. In 1942 pin tables were the chief attraction. In 1943 we went round tool shops, trying to buy some desired treasure, such as a small metal vice, or else took in the sights. On one awful occasion I was dragged to the very top of St. Paul's cathedral. We religiously counted all the steps—nearly four hundred, I believe, though it seemed three times that number—but I can't remember. All I recollect is that at every other flight on the way up to the dome the architect had provided a seat for the weary and someone else had later placed iron bars across these to prevent you using them. Obviously someone who had studied under Torquemada.

In 1944 the programme would be a good farce and an enormous lunch at whatever place could provide the most bulk in the way of eatables. On one of these excursions I gave him the experience of going back-stage instead of sitting in front.

While making for the station and home, we found ourselves near the stage door of a theatre at which I remembered that a friend of mine, Michael Shepley, was playing. In we went and found Michael in his dressing-room just starting to make up, the curtain being due up in half an hour or so. Jomfrey was vastly intrigued with the dressing-room and indeed the whole set-up, and watched Michael's every action as he started slapping grease-paint on his face. Innumerable questions were asked and Mike, the soul of kindness, started to tell the boy what all the different sticks of paint were for and how applied.

C

Soon he was actually illustrating their use: "If I want to make up as a business man fond of port I use this reddish one—thus . . ." And "These things are ' liners ' for drawing wrinkles and making yourself look older. For instance, in this play I'm a young man of twenty-five, but if I had to be, say, forty, I'd do this—and this—and this . . ."

"How do you look *really* old?" Jomfrey wanted to know.

"Oh, then you've got to do lots of other things—pouches under the eyes. . . . Like this. And crows-feet. . . ."

Jomfrey looked on entranced at this practical demonstration by an expert. So Michael continued . . .

And I must say it was really awfully sweet of him. He had just made himself the most convincing centenarian I've ever seen, when the call-boy rapped on the door with, "Beginners, please!"

Mike, it seemed, was opening the show as a juvenile in about two minutes . . .

I think he just made it—thanks to some frank soliloquy ad-libbing gagging by his opposite number. It was a great compliment to Jomfrey that, as an immediate one-man audience in the flesh, he had proved more attractive to Experienced Actor Shepley than a future audience of five hundred on the far side of the curtain.

In 1945, when he was seventeen, came the culmination of his London visits. I was working in my Air Ministry office one morning when I was rung up by my son who said: "Daddie, can you lend me some money?" Since he'd only gone back to Gresham's a fortnight before, I naturally asked what trouble he'd got into to have to ring up from Norfolk for money. No, he said, he was ringing up from Liverpool Street.

What? This was terrible! The boy had been expelled. I started to yammer into the phone. . . .

No, he said, he'd merely been to Cambridge to take the "Little-Go" Latin exam., and wanted his fare back to school.

"But," I protested, "didn't they provide you with money to go back?"

"Oh yes, daddie; but I spent it coming up to London for the day, and now I want some more to get back to Norfolk."

I told him to come along to the office, where I coughed up the sum required to get him back to the school at which he ought to have been already and for which I was paying. Dick Turpin would have had nothing on that lad.

As for Toni, I remember once seeing her off to school at Euston. The train drew in late and hordes of passengers started milling up and down in the usual wartime fight for seats. Compartments had been reserved for Toni's school (Howell's at Denbigh) but she and her companions, convinced that these would be at the front of the train, "because they were last time," had raced off there in an excited bevy. I found myself left alone, funnily enough just opposite the place where the Howells' compartments eventually drew up. Most people, seeing these were reserved, went elsewhere; not so two tough Canadian Commando sergeants, who scrambled in and spread kit and rifles and tommy-guns and throat-cutting knives and eye-gougers and so on possessively all over the place.

I pointed out the carriage was reserved. "To hell with that, there's a war on," they said in effect. I started to argue, but they were adamant. First come, first served: those who reserved the carriage ought to be there on time: action was their motto. They then lit up cigarettes and stayed aggressively put. One felt a tank attack would be needed to shift them.

"Of course you know it's reserved for a girls' school," I pointed out.

They may have been tough guys when Huns were about —but when it came to a girls' school. . . . I've never seen people move quicker and look more scared. I'm not certain one of them didn't jump out on to the line on the far side to avoid any chance of a head-on encounter.

Other London meetings with the children were of course during the Christmas holidays, when a pantomime outing was laid on. On one occasion we went to the Coliseum, where a friend of mine, George Gee, was playing. To give the kids a treat I took them round to his dressing-room afterwards, where George presented them all with autographed photographs of himself. These a-dorned our house for months after-wards and were proudly moved from position to position so often, that I got the im-pression there must be several dozen of the damned things. Everywhere I went I found George smiling at me, till I felt I couldn't bear to meet him in the Club ever again.

But on one famous occasion Toni made me realise just what being the father of a daughter really entails and at the same time gave me a most embarrassing experience.

This time we were seeing the circus at the Stoll Theatre and in the interval Monica and Felicity went off to buy refreshment. Jomfrey and Toni were left in the box, and I strolled off to the lobby to smoke a cigarette. Suddenly Jomfrey appeared towing twelve-year-old Toni by the hand. With all the scorn of a masculine fifteen years for feminine weakness, he announced simply, "Daddie, she wants to go again"—and faded out, leaving me to grapple.

I looked wildly round. No sign of Monica, but spotting a door appropriately labelled, I guided Toni thither. Of course it *had* to be bang opposite the queue for advance booking, a queue which, with nothing to do but wait and look about them, pretty soon sized up the situation as being worth their full attention.

It certainly was. Barely had the door closed behind the kid than she was out again. "Daddie," she announced, to the delight of all, "I haven't got a penny."

I produced one, re-launched the child and was about to slink off at high speed, when I remembered that Toni would never find her way back to the box alone. So there I waited, bright scarlet but trying to look nonchalant, while the queue openly giggled, and even those who'd moved up and bought their tickets stayed on to see if the finish would be as good as the beginning.

They weren't disappointed. In time out came Toni with a rush. "Here's your penny back, daddie," she shrilled proudly. "I put my foot in the door."

CHAPTER FOUR

AT FIRST, of course, I could not quite grasp that I was in future going to be a mere visitor in my own house—though I hoped a regular and welcome one—and that I should not have a tenth part of the time for gardening that I used to have. It certainly never occurred to me that I was not going to be able to cope with even the ordinary routine work which used to fall to my lot, apart from anything else. Thus, on one of my first real leaves, i.e., seven days, not forty-eight hours, I set myself gaily to carry on with the latest of the garden "expansions," upon which I'd been engaged when the R.A.F. reached out and scooped me in.

By expansion I don't mean that we were enlarging the garden in actual area: I refer to the gradual extension of civilised garden over the acre and a half of untamed fallow field that we had taken on in 1933 round the original cottage domain. For naturally we had not tried to make a complete garden in a few months by engaging a team of workmen captained by some expert landscape gardener, and then buying everything needed, from well-established delphiniums in flower up to full-grown trees with birds nesting in them. Apart from the fun of fashioning and planting your garden yourself, it is also much wiser to do it slowly. You are less liable to make mistakes for one thing—if you think things out beforehand; and mistakes in garden-making are not always easy to put right. A yew hedge, say, once planted, can hardly be moved three feet to the right in four or five years time, because you've suddenly decided you want more run-back for a tennis court.

So we had gone in for a lot of considering and measuring up and then planning out on paper just what we intended to do with each part of the new estate; and year by year we had brought a bit more under control. By the spring of

1939 we had only two patches unfinished—apart, of course, from the tennis court, which we could not yet afford and which in any case was a few months later switched over to Growing More Vegetables. One of these patches was still derelict; the other was in process of being transformed into a pond-cum-rockery, when war actually broke out.

The pond part had actually been finished and was in action, with things growing in it and all. It was—very roughly—the shape of a longish triangle with one short side. But it had looked so lonely and startled, plumped down as it was in a fallow patch of ground, that obviously something had to be done; moreover, there was also the mound of earth we'd excavated in order to bring it into being.

So I decided to flank the two long sides of the pond with rockery, which would give it, though only ten inches below ground level, a sort of sunken pool effect. The rockery would slope directly down to the water for about a third of the way along each side from the sharp end; at which points narrow stone-paved paths would lead in through the rockery from outside and carry on at the level of the pond and between it and the rockery down to the blunt corners. Here there'd be steps up to more paving at ground level along the inward curving short side. I then realised that I had a tree—a Siberian Crab—about seven feet away from the middle of this short side, and as luck would have it the curve of the side was such that it formed part of the circumference of a circle with the tree as centre. Obviously therefore I could carry on the paving right round the tree, leaving a circular bed in the middle, with the tree in the middle of that.

All this seemed to indicate a hell of a lot of paving and I toyed with the idea of buying up a street-load of London pavement; for I felt that it should be flat paving, not the rough stones which were all that were available locally. Then I thought of a better scheme. Paving stone would be expensive to transport; moreover, much of it would have to be broken up with much labour, since one could not easily fit large squares and oblongs round a small pond with a winding contour, or even round a circular flower-bed. So why not manufacture my own paving slabs out of concrete   Not only would it be cheaper, but one could make them in various interesting shapes. Never having heard of anyone who had done this before, I looked upon myself for the rest of the day as one of the world's great inventors. No doubt the idea was one of those original flashes which strike about three people in every six, but, as far as *I* was concerned, I considered myself in the same class as the fellow who first thought up the wheel.

Well, it was a history first of mistakes, and then of gradual labour-saving improvements.

I began by ordering a sack of cement and a load of sand, and meanwhile made half a dozen frames of wood, about one and a half inches deep, in different shapes—triangles, squares, parallelograms, rhomboids, anything my fancy dictated. My idea was to place them on the ground, fill them with cement—or rather sand and cement—and when the stuff had hardened, remove them, leaving a batch of one and a half-inch deep, but variously-shaped, paving stones. I could then use the frames for another lot and so on.

Off I went, choosing the concrete garage wash-down as being a suitable flat place on which both to put the frames and mix up the filling. I had the concrete mixed and the frames nicely laid out and was just starting to fill them, when along came Monica.

"Oh, are you going to do it there?" she asked.

"Why not?" I replied, bunging in the first shovelful in a workmanlike manner.

"O.K. with me," she said, "but when will they be dry enough to be moved?" I told her they'd take about two or three days. "Then do I drive over them when I take the car out this afternoon? . . ."

I got her point. In silence I took the first shovelful out

again, and moved the frames from the centre of the wash-
down to the side.

I soon completed the first batch and they were setting
nicely when Friar happened along. He asked how I was
going to move them. I told him they weren't too heavy
to lift and. . . . He looked at the sky and remarked to no
one in particular that, being concrete laid direct on to the
concrete of the garage wash-down, it seemed like they
might set on to it and be there for life; and that perhaps I
should have had wooden bottoms to the frames. . . .

I got *his* point. I just had time to break them up before
they became a permanency—a *monumentum aere perennius* to
my dim-wittedness.

The third batch I made with flat three-ply board from an
old tea-chest underneath; but when they were set and I
came to try and lift the frames off I found it quite impossible
because they had set to the concrete. So I had to knock my
carefully-made handiwork to pieces to get the slabs out.
However, I learned from this and for the next batch I only

nailed the frames together just tightly enough to hold the concrete inside. They were thus more easily taken apart; and I improved on this for the fifth edition by jamming the inner sides of the frames up against one another and holding the outer sides in position with heavy stones, so that I did not have to nail them together at all.

By now the Armstrong Home-Made-Paving Company was in full production, and the best brains of the board were being directed towards designing further improvements in both the product and the manufacturing processes.

First, it was noted that the slabs that were coming off the assembly lines were all too smooth to look well, whichever side up they were laid. The cement and sand mixture always set very even and sleek on the top owing to the water tending to come to the surface, however much I tried to roughen it; while the three-ply board made it equally flat on the bottom. This defect the Managing Director of the Company countered by scrapping the three-ply and using a layer or so of the thick paper from the cement sacks at the bottom of the frames instead. These had small wrinkles and curves in them, which the weight of the concrete never quite flattened out, and thus the slabs, though reasonably flat, did acquire a slight but attractive unevenness on one side, though still reasonably uniform.

Next we found that the cement set very white, which gave the paving, when laid, a rather phoney appearance, like imitation marble, or something in a Hollywood suburb. This problem we dealt with by mixing up colouring matter into the compound, red-lead, or yellow ochre, or even ground-up cubes of Reckett's blue, as used for washing linen. Not in great quantities, of course: we weren't after a vivid rainbow-hued path, but merely wanted to give a faint coloured tinge to the stones.[1] We soon found, however, that quite a large amount was needed to colour the whole

---

[1] It's as well to work your colour in *darker* than ultimately wanted, as the cement, which sets white, lightens it up considerably.

slab even faintly, whereas it was really just the surface that
needed it. So we overcame this trouble by mixing up only
a little of the coloured concrete and using it for the first
shovelful at the bottom of the frames, where of course it
subsequently appeared as the top of the slab.

So far, so good. But by then a new difficulty had arisen.
In my eagerness to get variation in sizes of slabs, I found I
hadn't thought about fitting them together, and this was
a jig-saw nightmare. Yet another improvement thus came
into being. I fitted them together as well as I could but
when I came to an awkward space to fill, I left it and made
a special frame to the size of that space. Thus I had a paving
stone made to measure and naturally fitting perfectly.
Bespoke tailoring, as it were.

From this came another improvement in our factory
procedure, which probably half of my readers have long ago
thought of and are only bothering to read on in order to
see how long it took this poor clot to tumble to it himself.
Instead of setting up frames and then pulling them to pieces
and then laboriously carrying the resultant slabs to the pond,
where I, of course, had to excavate or ram down the earth,
so that they could all be laid firm and level, I decided to
make them actually on the site.

In other words, I disbanded the frames entirely and used
the wooden side pieces *in situ* on the ground in any con-
venient pattern. It looked like a section of unsymmetrical
honeycomb and I filled the concrete straight on to the earth
in each section. Thus no actual levelling was necessary: as
long as there was a reasonable depth to fill, one and a half
to two inches, you just filled in till you were flush with the
rest of the slab. Any colouring, of course, to prevent the
dead-white effect of the cement, had to be worked in at the
top for this method, but this presented no difficulty. A
thing to remember is, when the cement is nearly set, to
wobble the dividing frame pieces slightly from side to side
so that they can be easily pulled out afterwards. Otherwise

you've got projecting wooden divisions as part of your path for life.

At this point a word of warning to any of you who may contemplate this making of paving stone on the spot. Children, particularly girls of three and seven, don't always know the difference between dry concrete and wet concrete, and step on the latter by mistake. Children, particularly *my* girls of three and seven, Felicity and Toni, did know the difference between dry concrete and wet concrete, and still stepped on the latter "by mistake." Result: deep footprints, fascinating to their makers but not to the maker of the slabs.

Mind you, it didn't need any Sherlock Holmes or Father Brown to work out the "whodunnit" angle, and proceedings were instituted against the two criminals. (Jomfrey had already gone back to school, or he too would have made his life sublime, and, departing, left behind him footprints on the sands of time.)

An amicable settlement was, however, arrived at. No more treading "by mistake" on wet slabs; and in return one official footprint each would be formally registered on a special paving-stone set apart for the purpose. Thus in the midst of the path round the pond you will see to this day the imprints of a five-inch and a seven-inch naked foot— flanked by one of the left front paw of Sally the bull terrier. On another slab is Jomfrey's imprint who, back from school later, had to be in it too. Fired by the whole idea Friar also surreptitiously registered on another one the imprint of his thumb and finger-tips. Every now and then he "notices" it in my company and says, "Wonder who that is?" and then fits his fingers in, apparently to make certain it's really him —or perhaps just to see if he's grown.

But to resume. As an advance on this direct-on-the-site method came my final labour-saving improvement. Already I had quite a lot of pavement laid—both the narrow pond-side paths and most of the three-foot wide one round the Siberian Crab; and already weeds of all sorts were pushing up through the interstices. I had earlier on tried to stop them by an intensive weeding campaign and then pouring liquid cement out of an old teapot all along the crevices between each stone to stop further intruders. But it wasn't a success—in case you have the same problem and are thinking of trying it. First of all, the cement mixture must be liquid enough to pour through the spout—and it's difficult

to get it into the right place without a spout.[1] This means it must be very watery and must be constantly stirred, or you have too weak a mixture, practically water at first, followed by thick almost unpourable cement at the end. Secondly, I found that since I did not want to fill the crevices right up—or otherwise the paving might just as well have

[1] One of those nice enamel quart-sized milk jugs borrowed from the kitchen might do, but I never got a chance to try. I was unfortunately detected borrowing it from the kitchen.

been laid solid and ugly at the start—I could not see whether gaps had been left or not. Thirdly, the cement did not bind well against the sides of the slabs owing to dirt having collected.

Result: through the weak and watery cement and through the gaps and along the sides of the slab weeds irresistibly forced themselves, and the job might never have been done at all.

Well, my final brain-wave, as I said, was this: When setting up the wooden partitions *in situ* for a new batch of paving, I raised them all, except those on the outer edges of the path, an inch or so above the bottom. Thus when I filled in the sections the concrete flowed under them and set in with the adjoining slabs. This gave the appearance of separate stones, when in fact all were linked underneath; yet weeds could not therefore come up between them.

As a matter of fact, as I said at the start of the chapter, I never was able to put this into effect, for by the end of that first leave I had reluctantly realised that there were limits to what I could accomplish in my garden and still do my R.A.F. work in London. A further improvement of the idea —for it was not always easy to raise the partitions off the ground without supporting them somewhere and so still having occasional gaps—might have been to lay the path solid and then while the concrete was still wet, stick the partitions about an inch or so down into it, thus achieving the same ultimate effect. But I'm not certain that wouldn't have been cheating.

Anyway by the time I had perforce downed tools and the Armstrong Home-made Paving Company had stated offici-ally it could accept no more orders owing to having to switch over to Government work, I had come a long way away from the day when I nearly built a row of permanent concrete "dragon's teeth," a veritable Siegfried Line tank defence, across the garage entrance.

CHAPTER FIVE

APART FROM the delight of getting back regularly to my home and garden—though not nearly as frequently as I would have liked—there was also the sudden sense of country peace—particularly at night. Although only fifty miles from London which might well be considered part of the front line, East Downing was practically out of it. We'd had in the early days a couple of bombs in a field in the next village, and a dud oil-drum incendiary a quarter-mile down the road, and a farm building a mile away set on fire by tracers from a German fighter who'd lost his way and wanted some daring exploit to report; and there was "the day the bomber came down in flames"—just on the Downs to the South East—plus, of course, the occasional German raids on Portsmouth, about twenty miles away. But that was about all. East Downing was hardly a military objective. Even the undiscriminating flying bombs, which in 1944 so frequently staggered complainingly over us, were on their way elsewhere.

True, there was one notable exception. I hadn't been in London very long then and one night there was a very big raid. It was directed at the City, and my part of Hampstead as usual, though receiving a few "overs," was more or less out of it. But it definitely was a maximum effort from the German side, because before going to the office in Aldwych next morning I took a walk down Fleet Street and counted seven large fires still raging between Australia House and Ludgate Circus. I thereupon thought I'd ring up Monica, who might be nervous on my behalf, and tell her I was O.K. Also, truth to tell, it was my first really big London raid, and I was rather proud of having been as near to it as I had been. Monica might even end up by being impressed.

47

I got through to East Downing and started off. "I thought you might like to know, darling . . ."

I was interrupted by excited twittering, as of a woman labouring under great emotion.

"Yes, yes, I know you must have been anxious: that's why I rang. Well, I'm . . ."

She continued to burble and I began to shout her down. "I'm quite *all right.* Just a couple several streets away, but . . ."

More excited remarks about the raid. Why couldn't she keep quiet and let *me* tell *her.* After all, *I* was the person who'd been in it. . . .

Well, as it turned out I wasn't. There had also been a blitz on Portsmouth that same night and a raider, in danger of being caught by one of our fighters, had been forced to shed its Molotov basket of incendiaries over, of all places, the tiny village of East Downing. Hedges had been blazing most of the night, a cowshed had been half-destroyed and the big house opposite had actually had two rooms completely burnt out. *And* our own Margarets even had had three incendiaries itself—one on the roof, which luckily bounced off merely breaking some tiles, and two quite close in the garden.

I at last put the receiver down, a somewhat embittered man. Monica had pinched *my* raid. I, in London, was made to feel like a chap who has been skulking in a safe area.

One bright point about it was that *three* incendiaries had been dropped in our garden. For I had three children, and so each got the remains of one bomb and there could be no quarrels. If there'd been only two we'd have had to ask the Hun to come back next night and drop another one—for the sake of peace and quietness in the home, and in the sacred cause of justice.

One of our own special garden incendiaries, by the way, had rather annoyingly dropped on the asparagus bed. As an asparagus addict, I would have preferred it almost anywhere

else Particularly as the asparagus had not been doing so
well in the first year of war and several patches had definitely
died on me. I don't why, because I had made it, according
to the best advice, only seven years previously[1] and I had
always understood that well-made beds lasted for a lifetime.
Provided, of course, you do not over-cut, particularly in the
first years. I have been frequently astonished by the number
of people—presumably eaters, not gardeners—who think
they can cut every head every year. You *must* leave some to
grow into fern, and so collect the sun and air above ground
which in summer and autumn it sends down to the roots to
maintain their vitality during the dormant months.

The only thing I can think of to explain the falling off,
is that we did not originally trench the site for the bed
deeply enough. We certainly went down and broke it up well,
but our sub-soil—soft chalky rock—was rather dishearten-
ing, and we could, I now feel, have gone even deeper. It
may therefore be that the foundation of the bed had slowly
clogged up, which would account for the trouble. Asparagus
in its natural state grows near a coast in sandy, and slightly
salty, soil. It therefore demands a well-drained bed: if
clayey or water-logged, the roots will ultimately rot away,
and this is what may have been happening to ours.

Another possibility is that, owing to not being earthed
up each year, the roots have got too near the surface, and
so have suffered from frost. But then there are two schools
of thought about this earthing up. Some gardeners regularly
each year drag up earth from the runway on either side of
the bed so that in time it becomes mounded up quite high.
I have seen beds as much as eighteen inches in height. Other
people just leave it, and as I found no definite advice to the
contrary in any of the books, that is what I did.

Anyway, whatever the cause, certain portions of my
asparagus bed had by 1941 "gone off," and in war-time

[1] Fully described in *We Like the Country* and so not repeated here. You lucky
people!

D

remaking was rather out of the question. Not that I felt
that it would be unpatriotic to spend time and energy on
a luxury food: on the contrary, I was one of that small
band of stalwarts who look on asparagus as a prime necessity
of life—including the melted butter. No, it was just that,
as explained in the previous chapter, I had by then realised
that the time at my disposal under the R.A.F. regime was
totally inadequate to undertake any garden expansions,
overhauls, re-plannings, or even renewals. Indeed, I wasn't
sure we would even be able to get through the mere routine
work and keep the garden in being at all. Certainly I would
have to cut out drastically all extra and unessential jobs,
and a lengthy campaign of repair and renovation to the
asparagus bed was one of them.

Another department of the Estate which also soon came
to be similarly affected by the shortage of man-power (me)
was the "annuals" section of our flower-garden branch
which Friar traditionally had always left to me to tackle.
You'd think, of course, that two days or so a fortnight
during March and April should be ample to scatter packets
of flower seeds here and there in beds or bare patches in
borders. In point of fact it wasn't all that simple. Half-
hardy annuals to begin with—nemesias, stocks, asters and
other old indispensables—need quite a bit of time spent on
them. They generally have to be started in boxes in the
greenhouse and pricked out and hardened off and planted
out and what-not. And even the hardy annuals, which are
not so fastidious and can be sown direct into the ground,
must not only have the site properly prepared for them, but
must be sown at the proper time—which frequently wasn't
the time when I could be there.

For although the directions on the packets normally say:
"Sow in spring in open ground where intended to flower,"
there's more in it than that. It's not so much the exact
month that matters, but the state of the ground. If the soil
is too wet the seeds rot, or are suffocated to death by soggy

earth; if the ground is still too cold they won't germinate.
Seeds sown when conditions are right, will be up and about
long before those sown earlier when conditions are wrong
—if these come up at all. Incidentally wind frequently offers
quite a problem—particularly when dealing with small
light seeds. You must sow on a fairly calm day, if you don't
want your plants coming up in long wind-blown swathes
many yards to leeward of the intended positions.

I must confess I was never particularly good at hardy
annuals, even when I had time and to spare for the job.
That "where intended to flower" seemed to mean something
different to them; for their intentions were rarely mine.
One of my annual intentions, for instance, was that they
should fill gaps in the herbaceous borders, but when I sowed
thickly to ensure that after thinning out there'd be good
plants just where I wanted them, they came up in such

close-packed serried ranks that thinning them was terribly tedious and invariably resulted in disturbing the roots of the ones I wanted to leave. If, on the other hand, I sowed thinly, so as to avoid too much subsequent elimination, they perversely came up even more thinly than that and I was still left with gaps in the herbaceous borders.

For the really important point about having a good, display of annuals is that they must be at the right distance apart. In other words, each plant must have ample space. Six fine well-developed fellows give a finer show than two dozen jostling each other into general debility and looking like a row of chronic invalids on a seaside promenade bench. Just consider what a single good clarkia, for instance, can do, if it gets real elbow room in good soil, as against the spindly single-stemmed specimens that have had to grow up in a large family. Over-crowding, indeed, is the cause of more failures than anything else and is a very common mistake— presumably because most people cannot harden their hearts sufficiently to pull up and throw away promising young seedlings.

Experts say that the correct distance apart for annuals is about half the plants' ultimate height, and that since you cannot sow each seed where you want it—or be sure of its coming up if you do—you *must* sow fairly thickly and thin drastically. You can avoid sowing too thickly, of course, in the case of very small seeds, by mixing fine sand with them and pretending you're sowing seeds thickly; but personally I always found that, mix sand in as I would, somehow the seeds shook down to the bottom and I had a final patch of solid-sown seed, with all the previous patches pure sand.

Another way of ensuring plants at the right intervals, and at the same time cutting out a lot of the subsequent thinning business, is to draw criss-cross parallel lines in the soil at the required intervals and at each intersection sow a very few seeds. (I forget who told me this—probably a

Senior Maths. Wrangler with a horticultural bent.) One seed from each group is sure to germinate and will be where you want it in relation to the others; and in any case you won't have to weed out more than a few seedlings from each bunch. Nice work—if you've time for it!

Personally, after many disappointments, I gave up to a great extent the sowing "where intended to flower" method —except for our usual irrepressibles, such as marigold, candytuft, lavatera, Virginia stock and Californian poppy, which had apparently adopted special corners of their own and came up year after year without turning a hair. Instead I tried sowing in sparse drills in a seed-bed, just as if they were young perennials or bedding plants or something valuable, and when they were a couple of inches high I moved them to where I definitely did intend them to flower, the right distance apart and all, without giving them a say in the matter.

It meant naturally a certain amount of care in moving: you should water the drill before you move them, so as not to break the roots, water the ground they're going into, and water them regularly afterwards. I did it quite successfully on the whole; but I rather think a "green finger" came into it; for I do seem to be one of those lucky people who can move things at almost any time and they somehow live. I remember that one year, in the middle of a bad drought, I moved four dozen annual larkspurs actually just coming into flower, and into a rather sun-scorched bed at that. Forty-seven of them lived: the remaining one died, but only because it was eaten down by a slug.

As a matter of fact there is a bit of a secret in this "green finger" (or "green thumb") stuff. And that is—water! I do genuinely believe there *are* certain people who have more success with growing cuttings and moving young plants about than others, but quite a lot of their success is due to the fact that for a long period afterwards they constantly and regularly water the things they move or plant.

Let me explain! A large proportion of non-gardeners-
and quite a few so-called gardeners, if it comes to that—are
under the impression that because plants grow in the soil,
the soil is the really important factor. This is not so.

The soil is only valuable in that it provides all the
various mineral salts the plant needs for full and vigorous
growth—nitrogen, potassium, phosphorus, iron, magnesium
and so on. (I'm ignoring the oxygen and carbon dioxide
which the plant extracts from the air: at the moment we're
only dealing with "below-decks".) The necessary minerals
are supplied to the plant as soil solutions by the water which
permeates the ground. But this water must be absorbed by
roots. Without its roots the plant won't get enough water
and so won't get all its many foods. A cutting will therefore
die unless it ultimately makes root.

But a cutting will live for quite a time in water alone,
as everyone knows—hence cut flowers on the dining-room
table and branches of flowering shrubs in the hall!—and
during this period the *instinct* of the stem (not of course of
a mere flower stalk) is to make roots to get the necessary
soil solutions, whether it goes so far as actually to do so
or not.

Water, therefore, comes before soil as the preserver of
plant life; what in effect you should be doing when you
stick a cutting in the ground is putting it in *water*, just as
you'd put it in a vase, but with soil all round so that the
rootlets, as soon as they start forming, can take over the
real job. (Naturally the lighter and finer the soil the easier
it will be for the rootlets to grow: to jam a cutting in
heavy clay is to put it in a strait-jacket.) Till these roots
form, therefore, you must water zealously and regularly.
Don't trickle water occasionally on the ground round the
cutting: send your mind down to its base and ask yourself
whether there's water *there*, just as you'd make certain that
they had enough water if they were in a vase in the hall.
Personally when I put a cutting in I make a little hollow

in the ground all round and keep filling that up with water
—or in the case of a row of cuttings, a little trench. Then I
know it is going straight down when it's wanted and not
running off sideways before it gets there.

If you want a proof of all the above, go out and cut some
two-foot lengths of climbing nasturtium and put them in
a glass jar of water. In a week you'll see that they are
sending out masses of white roots from the stems—though
they're not in soil at all. And if you were to fill the jar
with a mixture of fine sand and water they'd do the same;
you would, in fact, have "struck" nasturtium cuttings. But
if you fill the jar with soil and only water them sparsely
they'll soon die. It's the *water* does it.

Breaking away from this somewhat unusual but highly
temperate dissertation in praise of water, I'd like to return
to the subject of those annuals which in our garden—before
the war at any rate—used to come up regularly, self-sown,
in the same position.

Candytuft used to do this very nicely for us in a small
shrubbery, and by midsummer was a froth of white, lilac,
pink and carmine round the ankles of the deutzia, lilac,
buddleia and so on which lived there. It's a thing worth
trying, if you have a shrubbery that's fairly open—though
each year they should be freshened up with a packet of the
darker shades which are apt to go under to the hardier, or
tougher, white.

Calendula is another obliging customer; so is a thing
like *Gilia tricolor*—if you have any use for such a silly
little flower, rather like an impecunious third cousin of the
Virginia stock.

Another thing for which we used to reserve a couple of
small beds in which to do what it liked was eschscholtzia,
a flower I'm rather fond of. (Possibly because I'm rather
proud of being able to spell it: I know lots of people who
can't !) I used only to know eschscholtzia (right again, see!)
as a vivid orange flower, but it has many other lovely

colours as well.   The scarlet "Fireflame," for instance, "Carmine Queen," and "Gloaming" (rose and yellow inside, coral outside), and there are many delicate shades of pale yellow and cream and apricot-pink; while a brilliant golden bronze semi-double is "Toreador." These names, of course, are all from one particular nurseryman's catalogue, but almost exactly the same shades, with perhaps different names, will be found in other firms' lists.

Personally I used to keep the ordinary orange ones out of my two beds altogether.   They were really so vivid that they prevented appreciation of all the other shades.   Moreover, seeing that it was the more delicate shades I really wanted, I thought it advisable for another reason.   The orange ones are the original stock, the Californian poppy, and so, being common rough fellows, would gradually elbow their aristocratic, well-bred descendants out of the way.

Another point about keeping a small bed for eschscholtzias (I just can't miss!) was that, although theoretically annuals, the seedlings are often tough enough to stand the winter and so come into bloom very early and keep right on till the frosts (as Friar says) "put paid to they."

But the war, as I said, made me cut down on all but a few indispensable annuals, sweet-peas, asters and the rest, without which no garden, etc., etc.   I could not even carry on my usual custom of picking out each year one or two things from the catalogues which I'd never seen before, and often had never heard of before, and then watching what happened.   Sometimes I picked duds, that is, things that either weren't satisfactory when they did grow, or else, with me, didn't grow at all.   On the other hand, I often made quite a kill.

In 1938 I remember I discovered *Asperula azurea*, a pale blue branching flower, just right for going behind a line of low edging plants along a border.   Also *Limnanthes Douglasii*, six inches high with yellow-white flowers.   Both are fragrant and the latter is another of the things that seed themselves freely—a real find.

Bartonia aurea, one of my last recorded experiments, wasn't at all a success. I got it because it was "suitable for a poor dry soil," and I had just such a bed under the dining-room window. It was reputed to be a "free-blooming and showy annual with golden-yellow flowers"—and that's still all I know about it. Just hearsay, in fact! I tried three packets and not one plant came up.

Adonis flos was another thing I sampled, largely because the name attracted me. It's so unusual for any flower to have a second name that's at all simple and even natural. Just *flos*—the Latin for flower—instead of something like *Adonis rubrum nanum Prendergastii*.

And what is *it* like? Well, I just wouldn't know that either! Like Bartonia in one respect is all *I* can tell you— just doesn't come up.

CHAPTER SIX

I FULLY REALISE that this book is supposed to be about the same old triad as the others, i.e., house, garden and family but I cannot resist digressing here and there about London. After all, from the end of 1940 to 1946 I was actually in London more than five times as long as I was in Sussex, and so I think I can be excused for occasionally writing about my life there in what is ostensibly a country book.

Those early 1941 days in London are extraordinary to look back upon now. The 1939 and early 1940 period was probably even more extraordinary to compare, but then the "phoney" war was still on and it might almost be considered to be peace-time. But in 1941 the war was on in earnest. We were in the thick of the night bombing; the East End had been several times set ablaze; historic City buildings had been gutted; the sirens wailed almost nightly; there were heaps of rubble and chasms as yet unrepaired in many a well-known thoroughfare; theatres opened at five-thirty to thin houses; the dark streets rapidly emptied after seven o'clock, as workers went home to the suburbs out of the danger zone; many restaurants were closed in the evening, for the efflux of citizens from bombed London so reduced custom that it was hardly worth while keeping open; and England, well into her second year of war and under very genuine threat of invasion, was then standing alone in the whole civilised world against Germany and Italy's might.

Yet, even so, for Londoners the war had in some respects still hardly begun. It was not yet the grim business of make-shift, scarcity and discomfort—such as, I may point out, is still existing in peacetime 1946. True, income tax was already 10s. in the £, but twenty cigarettes were only one-and-sixpence, whisky was but sixteen shillings a bottle, and

the highest purchase tax was a beggarly 33⅓ per cent, instead
of double the article's price, if it were rated as a luxury.
And there were no austerity meals or clothing coupons or
sweet rations; taxis were obtainable without much difficulty; you could take a long railway journey without the
certainty of having to stand in the corridor if you weren't
there an hour beforehand; for many months to come there
would be sherry at Henneky's at 1s. 1½d. the large glass;
laundry was still delivered once a week; there was a basic
petrol ration which, small though it was, you could use as
you liked; and shopkeepers did not seem to consider that
your expression of a desire to buy something from them was
a studied insult to be met with either sarcasm or open
rudeness. You could even order a bottle of wine in a
restaurant and find that it was good wine at a reasonable
price, not *vinegar ordinaire* at two pounds the bottle—if
obtainable. Indeed on New Year's Day, 1941, my brother
and I, prior to dining at my mother's house in Hampstead,
walked down to the local and came back with a celebratory
bottle of quite reasonable Beaune bought over the counter
for five shillings.

Those were the days. Why, in 1940 one could even still
meet quite a lot of British people in Hampstead. In 1942
and 1943 of course it was different. I am quite open to con-
tradiction, but we in Hampstead did seem to have acquired
more than our fair share of foreigners. Going home to
Hampstead by Tube each night was rather like taking a
journey to a foreign land—I kept wondering if my passport
was in order and if I had remembered to change my English
money. We called Belsize Park Station "The Gate to the
Orient."

Outside that station, by the way, there was a seller of
Sunday newspapers and waiting in the queue was always
philologically and phonetically instructive: "Zonday
Taimes?" "Heggspresh," "Der Gronicle, pliz." "I vant ze
Pipple," "News of de Voild?" By the time I'd got to the

head of the queue and said "*Sunday Express*, please," the paper-seller (British) was practically in the mood to shake hands and say, "Dr. Livingstone, I presume?"

Indeed one felt that if one died in Hampstead one would like to be buried locally and have on one's tomb, "There is some corner of a foreign field that is for ever England." It'd hardly be an exaggeration, for I remember, when walking up the hill from the Tube late one evening, I once out of curiosity asked the first seven people whom I met the way to Whitestone Pond. Believe it or not, I only got one answer that wasn't in broken English. And what it *was* in I don't know—probably Yiddish, with a Polish off-break.

I say Yiddish, but whether the majority of these war-time Hampsteadians really were Jews or not it is unfair to state categorically without full proof. There is rather too much of a tendency to assume that all dark-haired foreigners speaking in broken English are Jews, and then to run them down. Unfortunately, however, it cannot be denied that the less well-off Central European Jews who came to live in England during the war years were not the best of citizens. (Probably the poor devils had never had the chance, and were just living in the only way they knew.) But they always seemed to be after something for nothing, dodging regulations, getting in first somewhere, oiling through loop-holes, with little sense of responsibility or gratitude to the country which, admittedly not their own, was at least giving them sanctuary and enabling them to earn a living, away from the insane brutality of Hitlerism. Of course it is easy to generalise, but in three cases out of four when someone behind me in a queue has gradually come up alongside and then gradually tried to get in front, it has been unmistakably a somewhat unprepossessing foreigner of a Jewish cast of countenance.

But to get back to Belsize Park. I remember getting out there one black night. I had just switched on my torch when an attractive and imploring young feminine voice at my shoulder said—in broken English: "Oh pliz, you 'ave a torch, may I valk with you up the hill?" Naturally, before replying, I switched my torch casually on to her, but the rest of the picture didn't live up to the voice. She was about four foot high with the figure of a tennis-ball and rather a fine black moustache. No wonder her reason for wanting to walk with me was my torch, not the fear of being molested. She'd have been safe anywhere.

So off we set up the hill and I soon got pretty annoyed. My battery was on its last legs and in any case I was accustomed to switch it on at intervals rather than keep it on the whole time. But the first time I gave it a rest, during a clear stretch of pavement, a pathetic "Oh pliz, the light!" made me switch it on again. On top of this, Fraulein Tennisball pit-potted along on her high heels at less than a mile an hour. My battery was obviously for it.

At last I got hard-hearted and decided to ditch her. Batteries were, as usual, hard to replace; and one had to conserve them. So some while before I'd reached my road I said, "I'm sorry, I turn off here. Good night." "Good night, pliz—thank you moch!" replied the damsel and continued up the hill, switching on her torch as she went. She, too, knew well that one had to conserve batteries.

And then from further behind came voices: "Danke-schön," "Goombye, sir," and so on, as my unrealised comet's tail also dispersed, *also* switching on its torches. Well perhaps that part of the story isn't true, but it makes a good finish. And it *has* happened to me elsewhere. Indeed, to be honest, there are few of us who at one time or another have not been grateful to someone with a bright torch just in front going the same way and at the same pace as oneself.

Of course I may be doing an injustice to a lot of foreigners. On the other hand, during the last five years, England has had so many of her sons out of the country and so many other nations' sons in it, as fugitives from persecution, that she can hardly be accused of lacking

sympathy with the oppressed—even though there may
be no point of view as to just how far that sympathy
should go. At which point, I recount without hesitation,
and completely without a moral, a simple little story.

A German Jew went to a railway station booking office
and said: "Third return, Blackpool, please. How much?"
The clerk said: "Forty-five shillings and sevenpence. "

Back flashed the Jew: "Give you thirty-five bob."

"No, sir, the fixed price of a third-return Blackpool is
forty-five and seven."

"All right, all right, I'll mek it forty bob."

"But don't you understand?" snapped the clerk. "The
price is *forty-seven and six*."

"Huh! *I* see! Anti-semitic, hey?"

And here's a reminiscent little verse, called "Hampstead,
1942":

> Climbing streets and bijou houses,
> Gardened mansions girt with walls,
> Heath where dogs and children scamper,
> Tree-lined roads where blackbird calls—
> And the lisp of Hampstead English
> Gently breaking as it falls. . . .

Still, even though the British did rather seem to be
playing the rôle of an underground resistance movement in
Hampstead, I always had a soft spot in my heart for that
particular borough. I'd lived there with my parents, near
what the Tube porters used to call "*Ssscot*tage," before, during
the last war, and soon after being married I had lived in
Rosslyn Hill for about seven and a half years. In fact both
Jomfrey and Toni were born there—in a little red-brick,
rather jerry-built house, with a garden the size of a small
bath-towel.

Mention of this garden—if you care to call it that—
makes me recall how sublimely ignorant I was in those

Rosslyn Hill days of anything to do with gardening. I have since gone from the sublime to the ridiculous in that I am now merely ridiculously ignorant; for at least I have vague glimmerings of how much there is to know and how much of it I don't. But at that time—before of course the 1928 Margaret Cottage days when I first caught horticulture —I remember I would cheerfully buy a packet or so of seeds, and empty them haphazard over a patch of ground, regardless of whether it had been wet-trodden and then baked as flat and hard as the side of a battleship, or whether it was large, rough, unbroken clods of acid London soil. It was earth, and seeds grew in earth; and that was enough for me. I little realised that about ten years later I should be writing a weekly gardening page in a London daily.

To be frank, I was perfectly well aware that I had not been engaged by the paper to give out any horticultural lore I possessed. For many years they had had on the staff one of the best-known gardening experts in England and he was the horticultural lore-giver. Moreover, he was the fellow who, as well as attracting readers, also attracted advertisers —which any Editor will tell you is far more important. My particular function was apparently that of "clown-dog," the bloke who did things wrong. The Expert wrote about Gardening in General: I was there to write about my own particular small garden at Margarets. The Expert's target was the achievement of perfection—what one should do and the right way to do it. I had no target at all except a weekly report—interspersed with digressions on subjects only remotely horticultural—on what I personally had actually been doing that week, inevitably miles from perfection and often in quite the wrong way. As a result, my column was simply full of human error and most weeks something like this appeared: "In my last article I was telling you of an idea we had about taking cuttings of *Cydonia japonica*; well, I'm sorry, but it doesn't seem to work." No readers seemed to mind, or wrote in to say I'd wilfully misled them: I think

they'd got me sized up right at the start and for real information, as opposed to light reading, they studied the Expert's
page.

I did receive a good many letters though, and so far from
teaching people anything about gardening, I got lots of
tips myself; probably I'm the only bloke who ever con-
ducted a gardening page *in statu pupillari*. I was also
frequently sent seeds by enthusiasts—not professional
seedsmen, but amateur gardeners who wrote lyrically that
if I didn't grow *those* I didn't grow anything. In this way,
I remember, I was first introduced to *Anemone pulsatilla* (or
Pasque Flower)—the lovely mauve spring-flowering anemone
with the golden heart. It sounds as though it ought to be
difficult to raise from seed; actually it grows most easily:
a handful of it—rather like thistledown—put in a box, is a
mass of seedlings before even the weeds can come up, and
that's saying something.

Another gift was a packet of seeds of *Meconopsis Baileyi*,
the Tibetan Poppy from the Himalayas, or the Himalayan
Poppy from Tibet. This also has a golden centre and blue
petals, a clear sky-blue, which some people say is the most
attractive blue in the garden. It grows to three foot high
and the blooms are often four inches across. *Meconopsis*,
however, I completely failed to grow, in spite of giving it
as much care as would make a new-born baby look neglected.
To rear it successfully you must have *fresh* seed, and this
should be sown in February in a box in a cool greenhouse,
covered with glass and later shaded from sun. The soil
should be light sand and leaf-mould mixed. Then you prick
out into other boxes or pots, let them recover and make
root, and then out they can go in the garden. That is,
assuming they are up: the seeds sometimes take a long time
to germinate. Some people, I believe, sow them direct in
the garden as soon as the seeds are ripe, about August, and
leave them there all winter, pricking out when they come
up, or *if* they come up, next spring. They like a moist, shady

E

site, and it's a good plan not to let them flower the first
year; then they are the more likely to establish themselves
properly as hardy perennials. One of these days I must try
again: it is a lovely flower.

My correspondence, however, was not only from passers-

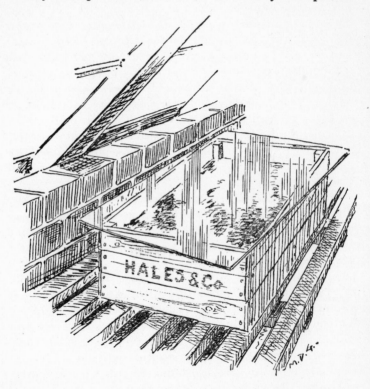

on of tips, or donors of seed. I used frequently to get into
arguments with readers, but never apparently on any real
gardening subject. Letters arguing about the best method
of combating downy mildew on antirrhinums no doubt
all went into the Expert's post bag—and very rightly too—
whereas I would find myself being taken up on one of my

only vaguely horticultural digressions. One such I remember
was over the correct way of pronouncing "gladioli." I think
I'd said that value should be given to the "glad eye"—
glad*i*oli; and at once I got heated letters pointing out that it
should be gladi*o*li.

One old lady of eighty threw quite a new light on the
question. She said that many years ago, when living about
fifty miles from Chicago, her husband, who was also
British, had made a typically English garden. It developed
apparently into quite a show-place and all the local towns-
people became obsessed with the idea of having one like it.
The ironmonger reported that he had sold more spades, hoes,
etc., in one month than in the past year. When Americans
take a thing up, they do it in a big way. It seemed, however,
that they had never seen gladioli before and my correspondent sold thousands of them to keen amateurs. But when
it came to pronouncing them, the ensuing argument
threatened to split the community. At last the local ladies,
who had of course formed a Gardening Club, called a special
meeting to decide the question. After accenting the wretched
word on every single syllable it was decided by a majority
vote to call it "gladi*o*la." The unofficial feminine termina-
tion was certainly a rather original touch, but at least it
made the flower eligible for a women's club.

As a matter of fact the dictionary allows you to accent
either the "i" or the "o," so what's it all matter? Some
people call the things "gladdies" and get over it like that.
My Mr. Friar occasionally says something like "gladdias"
and we talk at cross-purposes for some while—till I realise
he's referring to gaillardias. . . .

To be frank, it was always worth while in my articles
throwing out some slightly controversial statement, or
mentioning some popular superstition; as the result produced material for a paragraph in a later article. I once
stated that I had been told that you can't get yellow crocuses
to flower in bowls indoors. They come, I wrote, to the point

where you can just see from the bud that they're going to be yellow and then they wither, leaving you with only whites and purples. The yellow ones you *do* see in houses are ones that are grown out of doors up to the point of flowering and then brought inside, where, albeit pretty sulky at being fooled, they decide to carry on as planned.

Well, I got a lot of letters about that. Readers everywhere seemed to have their rooms ankle-deep in yellow crocuses, one lucky lady stating she had seventy-six in a seven-inch bowl. Another lady, having dealt with the colour-bar question, added gratuitously that whether yellow, white, or purple, a useful tip to ensure perfect flowering of crocuses was to snip an eighth of an inch off the top of the flower sheath just as the bud is showing in the green. We tried this and it certainly worked.

In conclusion, I can't resist quoting one delightful letter I received from an old man. I had been speculating on the origin of the word "spit," meaning a spade's depth of soil— whether it was related to the spit used in cooking, or the forty-bob-penalty spit; for these two words, if you look at your dictionary, are differently derived. The old man had read my maunderings and had apparently decided to give me his views. His letter, below, is quoted verbatim and needs a little co-operation from the reader, as the sole punctuation employed was but five casually placed full stops.

Dear Sir Being a reader of your G. notes in the paper permit me to give you my suggestion on the spade thrust deep or spit. Thrust as the swordsman thrust and spit his adversary through or as the Roast beef of old England used to be roast on the spit in the roast jack rotating and basted in its fat with the wooden Basting Spoon even the vulgar habit of spitting do we not thrust it out of the mouth spit the old roast beef of ol england is all Baked these day not roast is there any bearing on your question. Dear Sir a Loco engine driver friend once showed me a mystery on his allot with bricks and mortar built a frame first brap (?) mushroom bed not a mushroom in the frame but on outside walls like rosettes full. Now the solution I think all mushrooms are fluid in first stages and had ozzed throuh the wall allthough it was hard tight and grown hard after and don't lift as believed. Dear Sir another mushroom mystery the fairy ring wonder to many simple enough the ring is caused by rabbits The Doe in season lobs around in the same ring the buck in close attendance behind her often another buck vanquised in another ring outside the first one or even a third in another all keeping time all parting with urine and dung trod in the ground enriched grows darker grass and sometimes the fairy ring mushes. Sir I have had sometimes a thrill moonlight night or more fright when happening on the ring in the making mad dance all reared up on hind legs ears cocked little fairies 3 feet high gone a white tail A scared man.

73 years old country man now Town

Cheerio waste paper basket.

CHAPTER SEVEN

THE DAYS are long past when nations sent off their armies to wage war for them—like a Football Club arranging a fixture for the team—while everybody else then sat back in the grandstand in comparative comfort. Inexorably the war involved the whole nation from top to bottom, and drew ruthlessly upon all available national resources. On top of the direct bombing, therefore, the civilian population had also to endure a myriad restrictions, improvisations, substitutes and economies. Over the whole of normal life in England slowly descended the depressing mantle of war scarcity. Scarcity of materials, labour, of service, of transport. Goods were no longer sold to you: you had to *buy* them—if you could. You had to gird your loins and go out to search for what you wanted—only to find half the time you couldn't get it even then. You got into the habit of peregrinating feverishly round shops, cajoling in familiar neighbourhoods, nervously ingratiating in unknown territory, bluffing here, putting up a "helpless" act there. You were apt, when walking down a street with a friend, to break off a conversation with an abrupt: "Excuse me, I'll just pop in here on the off-chance. . . ." And you were as pleased as hell whenever the chance came off and you managed to secure some of whatever it was that was scarce—even though your need was not an immediate one.

And that last is the way Black Markets come into being; it's the thin end of the cloven hoof, as it were. For though you personally were only following your natural instinct to get something when you had the chance, rather than waiting till you actually wanted it and then perhaps failing, others did not stop there. The world has got pretty far to go before it can eliminate those people with no social sense who *will* try to get more than their share whenever they can,

so as to obviate any chance of *their* running short, whatever
may happen to any one else. And there'll always be some of
these who take the next logical step of purposely setting out
to get more than their share, not just to avoid the risk of
running short; but deliberately to dispose of it at a profit
to those less slick and with more social conscience. I'm not
even certain that the housewife who was once in 1942 heard
saying to a friend, "You'd better buy up all the dried eggs
you can now, dear, as I hear they'll be scarce after the war,"
was not taking the first downward step.[1]

Nevertheless I always experienced a great feeling of pride
if I managed to find and bring back from London something
Monica wanted and could not get locally. Rather like a
puppy bringing a slipper into the drawing-room. The
trouble about scarcities, however, in this last war was that
you could never quite keep tabs on just what *was* scarce at
any given moment—and so were constantly getting had.
Take, for instance, high-tension batteries for our wireless
which was only a portable. These were constantly unobtainable in Midfield, and so in response to an urgent
appeal I would start an intensive scouring of the wireless
shops of London and on my next return home would
probably lug back my catch with aching arms. Then one
day I arrived with my prize, only to find that during my
twelve days' absence batteries had for some obscure reason
started practically to grow on bushes in our neighbourhood.
A friend of Monica's, commissioned to try for one in
Chichester, had returned triumphant; Monica, with no real
confidence in the other's success, had snaffled one she unexpectedly saw in Midfield; and someone else had phoned to
say that, referring to our almost forgotten order of four
months previously, they were holding one for her. With
mine that made four all at once; and had I known I could
have saved my right arm being permanently stretched to
three inches longer than the left.

[1] A joke in 1942 which became a grim reality in 1945.

Another time—Christmas, 1944—toilet paper vanished from the locality almost over-night, and I in London was sent an S.O.S. to go out and see what the Great Metropolis could provide. I spent a week of fruitless and unromantic searching in my spare time—one obliging chemist actually offered to put my name on his list of waiting clients, but I said, to his surprise, I couldn't wait—and then suddenly the R.A.F. Warrant Officer, who worked with me in my Air Ministry office, and was helping me in my hunt, came rushing in in great excitement, like a sentry in a beleaguered garrison reporting imminent relief. He had seen some in a small shop in Finsbury and, using what urgent excuse I just wouldn't know, had bought three rolls. As I was off on Xmas leave next day I took them home and hung them formally on the Xmas tree: "For the family, with love." Never was a Christmas present more enthusiastically or hilariously received. All the same, the hiatus had apparently been bridged, so Monica told me, by press-ganging the three children, arming them with scissors and copies of *The Times*, and giving them each a target figure of so many sheets by tea-time.

Another time cigarettes would be the trouble. For some months they'd be fairly easy to obtain; a few months later, if you noticed a man taking one from a new packet you'd trace his footsteps back to find out where he'd got them.

Or else there'd be a period in which every tobacconist sported a "No Matches" sign almost as permanent as the name on the shop, and for any lucky man to strike a match was the signal for three people next him to whip out cigarettes and make up a foursome. Then in desperation you'd go into your local shop and over the "No Matches" sign would hoarsely whisper a frantic plea as between friends for just one little box from under the counter—and would be given three. The drought was over, the rains had come, and the shopkeeper had merely forgotten to take the sign down.

Or one summer every one would be officially told to order as much coke as one could stock, in order to avoid a rush of orders in the cold weather and consequent shortage due to transport congestion. When this happened—in, I think, 1943—we at Margarets obediently rang up our coal merchant and patriotically booked an order for a complete truck-load, which we realised we could dump in a derelict patch by the chicken-run. Within two months stringent rationing set in—no one to order more than two pounds of coke, if he'd already got anything over fourteen ounces in the cellar, or something of the sort—and in the middle of this our long-awaited truck turned up in full view of every one in the village. We only just escaped being lynched for blacketeering.

Or beer would suddenly be, as they say in City circles, in short supply. "No bitter," or "Only mild-and-bitter," the young lady would snap haughtily to a point above and beyond your right shoulder. But I, who wanted just one half-pint of bitter, could never understand the reasoning which led to my not being allowed it as a half-pint by itself, *but* being allowed it as half of a full pint of mild-and-bitter. I used to ask if I couldn't have a pint of M. & B. served in separate glasses so that I could leave the mild which I didn't want; but I always received a truculent refusal and never really got the logic of it.

Whisky, of course, seemed to be permanently short in the war, though not being a whisky-drinker I could afford to down my beer and watch with amused tolerance the *sotto voce* remarks across the bar, and the curt "no spirits"; or to favoured regulars the quick measuring out, plus obvious soda splash, under the counter, followed by a fulsomely mendacious "Your dry ginger ale, sir."

In this whisky-shortage connection, I shall never forget seeing a film called "The Lost Week End," the tale of three days in the life of a dipsomaniac. In the picture, readers will perhaps remember, the principal character downed enough

whisky to float the *Queen Mary*, while the audience got steadily thirstier and more envious. But when the Good Brother discovered a hidden bottle and, by way of saving Bad Brother from temptation, poured it away down the sink, the audience raised such a wail of pain and horror as I have never heard equalled, and strong men had to be led out weeping bitterly.[1]

Of course subterfuge in drink-winning was by no means entirely produced by the war. Licensing laws had already seen to that. I remember leaving the Savage Club in Adelphi Terrace one night some ten years or so ago at the same time as two friends, B. C. Hilliam ("Flotsam") and Charles "Jock" Prentice of Drury Lane musical fame. They asked if I was going to the tube, and I said, no, I had a room that night at a hotel nearby. A meaning look flashed between them and they each took an arm and said, " *We'll* see you there, old man."

I said I was perfectly capable of going there by myself, but they said, oh, no, no, it was no trouble at *all*, they *liked* my company, they wanted to make *sure* I'd got my room booked, and so on. It then dawned on me that what they really wanted was a final drink, but that it was Past Closing Time; nevertheless I, as a resident, could lawfully order one at the hotel. One, or more likely three. Oh yes, of course they were coming with me.

"But I don't *want* a drink," I protested plaintively.

They had the answer to that one.

"*We* do," they chorused.

In we went—there was no shaking off those two. We contacted a little nut-cracker-faced night-porter and they nudged me to do my stuff. They then stood thirstily in the background. So I began by smiling at the crusty little porter and asking tentatively if I could get a drink.

"You staying in the 'otel?"

[1] I saw this film with Tommy Watson, the Hearst correspondent over here. As we came out he said: "Tony, there are only two things we can do now, sign the pledge or go and have three doubles." I forget which we did.

"Oh, yes, yes. Room 521."

"Oh!" He checked it. "Thassright!"

"Then—er—can we have three bottles of beer?"

"*They* staying in the 'otel?"

"Well, not exactly. But they're my guests."

"*You* can 'ave a drink. But *they* can't," he said uncom-promisingly.

"Oh, surely if *I* order the three and pay . . ."

"'Gainst rules."

I resumed, even more persuasively: "Look here, perhaps it *is* against rules. But is it against rules for me to buy *you* a drink too?"

The first signs of weakening began to set in. "You know as well as I do I oughtn't to do it."

"Oh yes, I know. But they're frightfully thirsty . . ."

"The lor, you know, don't reely allow it . . ."

"They're personal friends of mine and it's only *just* after closing . . ."

"We—ell," he said doubtfully. . . .

And it was at this point, when indications of co-operation, albeit highly reluctant, were making themselves definitely apparent, that Flotsam, in the background, got impatient and decided I wasn't handling this thing in the right way. He pushed to the front.

"Look here," he said genially to the little hall porter, "I'll tell you who we are. We're not just ordinary members of the public trying to get a drink. It may interest you to know that this" indicating Jock—"is Mr. Charles Prentice, Musical Director of Drury Lane Theatre, and this is Mr. ANTHONY ARMSTRONG, author of *Ten Minute Alibi*, which ran two and a quarter years in London, and I—ahem —am *FLOTSAM* of " *FLOTSAM AND JETSAM*."

The man was quick on his cue and all my tactful pre-liminary spadework went down the drain.

"Oh, are you?" he said scornfully. "Well, I'm the *QUEEN OF SHEBA* and you don't get no drinks."

And we didn't. Not even me.

Resuming, another result of all the war shortages of everything you seemed to want was to make you realise your dependance on the complex machinery of twentieth, century civilisation. For the impact of war invariably sets civilisation back both materially as well as spiritually. It lowers standards all round. It cuts off the supply of luxuries and limits the supply of necessities. Moreover, the demarcation line between a luxury and a necessity is often a very fluid one. The further civilisation progresses, the more the luxuries of life develop into necessities. Half of what are now necessities to a Londoner are still unimagined luxuries to a savage. Half of what the savage needs would be luxuries to the primitive caveman, who had to work and fight hard to win the bare necessities for actual existence.

Thus the war conditions threw down a sort of challenge to your ability to exist by *getting* things for yourself. Primitive man, you argued, didn't rely on having things brought to him: he went all out to get them and if he couldn't, he *made* them for himself. And so, metaphorically drumming on your chest and keeping a wary eye open for sabre-toothed tiger, you set about improvising or actually manufacturing things for yourself. Not all of them, of course, were necessities, but they were things you wanted. And the idea was right: the instinct to rely upon one's own resources was there just the same.

Sometimes too one really Got Results. Here's a very minor example, but I look on it as Caveman Armstrong's most successful war-time improvisation. The principal credit, however, must go to Jomfrey for the original idea.

I had the misfortune to lose—or have pinched— a nice leather, oiled-silk-lined sponge-bag, which was in constant use as I travelled to and from home or R.A.F. Stations. Even though it was 1944, I lightheartedly thought I'd buy another. I argued that surely things like sponge-bags couldn't be " on active service" or "in battle-dress till the end of the war," the usual explanation of why nearly everything else one wanted to buy was unobtainable.

My inquiries, of course, were everywhere met with a pitying stare. Finally one day, when Jomfrey happened to be up in town on a visit, we passed a luxury chemist in Piccadilly, one of the few in London I hadn't tried. Still determined not to be beaten, I went in. Actually they had one, they said, but when produced it turned out to be a shoddy unlined bag made of some stuff like Japanese imitation American Cloth. The price was a mere 15s. 6d. Even so I was toying with the idea, but when I asked, "Is it waterproof?" the man smiled in a superior fashion—as though I'd asked if it could sing hymns—and replied, "Oh, no, sir, that material isn't *waterproof*!" This seemed to me to disqualify it as an efficient sponge-bag, and I went out.[1]

Then as Jomfrey and I a little later passed a large ladies' shop near Leicester Square, he suddenly nudged me and said, "Look, daddy! Sponge-bags!"

I looked. There was quite a big window display of more or less triangular oiled-linen objects with elastic tops. They were marked "Bargain Line! Babies' Mac Drawers. Only 1s. 11¾d."

"Mummie could sew the legs up," explained my resourceful child. I replied, "Son, you've got something there," and in we went, pushing our way through a surge of shopping women.

Jomfrey by then was highly embarrassed at being confronted with the practical application of his ingenious suggestion, but I was on my mettle and not going to be beaten.

A tall lady floor-walker with a high net collar floated up, amusedly tolerant of these two lone males.

[1] I had an even better experience on similar lines in 1945 when I asked a jeweller if the luminous paint which had worn off the hands of my wrist-watch could be replaced, or was it, like everything else, unobtainable. "Oh, we can *get* luminous paint, sir," he said, to my surprise and delight, adding, however, "But I don't advise it. It isn't luminous."

"Babies' Mac Drawers, please?" I asked briskly.

"Straight through, sir, for Babies' Mac. . . . *What* did you say?"

I repeated, in authoritative tones. She eyed me strangely and then directed me in a subdued voice.

With a rather hot-faced Jomfrey on my heels, I beat another female floor-walker into submission and arrived at a counter where many women were buying incredible things. All eyes were on us, but in the tone of one who's been doing it for years, I drawled to the salesgirl: "I want to see some Babies' Mac Drawers, please."

She merely gulped. I suppose Squadron-Leaders in uniform didn't often come her way with that request. More briskly I repeated: "I want to see Mac Drawers, please."

The moment I'd said this of course, I realised it was just on the cards the firm might have a Scots sales-manager or something, and she might reply: "Mr. Angus McDrawers? Certainly, Sir!" But she only maintained a hunted silence.

"I saw them in the window," I explained haughtily. "A bargain line at one-and-eleven-three, I understand."

She too was cowed, and silently produced the objects. Jomfrey had been right. With the leg holes stitched up, I would have a soignée little sponge-bag, and only two bob instead of 15s. 6d. at the chemist's. This recalled to my mind one more point, and it was here I made my first mistake, after having dominated all these women and carried out an embarrassing mission with decision and success.

"Are they waterproof?" I asked keenly.

"What would *you* think?" retorted the damsel—and, snatching up my purchase, I left the shop, followed by gales of feminine laughter. Still, I'd got—and still have—the perfect war-time sponge-bag.

With some of our improvised or home-made substitutes, however, we did not have so much luck. Take, for instance, even such a little thing as fly-papers. I should have thought that these, as tending to prevent contamination of food, would have been considered almost necessities; and supplies would have been kept fairly regularly on the market. But in the summer of 1944 when flies were extremely plentiful— particularly in our kitchen—fly-papers, it seemed, were un- obtainable locally. Monica having reported the fact, I once more assumed my now well-known rôle of almost magical provider from London of luxuries unobtainable in the country, and started dropping into shops in Hampstead to collect a store of fly-papers and "surprise the Little Woman."

There were only two difficulties. My first was: *what* sort of shop sells flypapers? I found myself baffled. The grocer said it was the chemist; the chemist said it was the hardware man; the hardware man said it was the oil shop five doors down; the oil shop five doors down was shut and boarded up, and when at last the owner was run to earth he expressed the opinion that flying bombs rather than flies were his trouble at the moment.

So I invaded a fresh neighbourhood and then another and at last realised the second of my two difficulties. This was simply that even in London there *were no* fly-papers. I had to admit defeat.

Then one evening I turned up a little book—"One Thousand Odd Jobs About The House," or words to that effect. Amongst the jobs it told the reader how to make fly-papers; I forget the other nine hundred and ninety-nine. The briefing was: One ounce of powdered resin to three fluid drachms of colza oil, to be heated on the hob, well mixed by stirring and then brushed on pieces of paper. It immediately revived the old primitive spirit. If one couldn't *get*, one must *make*. So when next old Caveman Armstrong was home he grasped his stone axe firmly and went on a foray in the jungle of Midfield, peering through his tangled eyebrows for a wild chemist's shop.

I found one and bought the doings, but not having a hob I put the mixture on the "Aga" in a jampot inside a boiling

JOHNSON'S

CHEMIST

-MICHAEL D LOBLAM.

saucepan. It looked very unhopeful from the start. The tablespoonful of oil or so seemed such an infinitesimal drop in the resin, which took hours to melt. And when it did, stir as I might, the compound was still so stiff that, though I'd sacrificed my best paintbrush, I couldn't "brush it on" the paper strips at all, but had to dab it in splodges, and hope the flies when approaching to land would not distinguish between those parts of the airfield which were O.K. and those which were U/S (unserviceable). I did five pieces, hung them up immediately in the kitchen and formally declared them open for clients.

Having waited five minutes without a single customer, though the flies swarmed on everything else, including me, I got bored and went away. Perhaps they were merely shy of sadistic onlookers.

I came back after half an hour, expecting to find my papers as dark with trapped flies as a bonnet with black bugles. . . .

Something must have gone wrong. Either I'd boiled the stuff instead of just heating it, or had got the ingredients wrong—too little oil perhaps, fluid drachms instead of fluid oz.—but not a fly showed on the glistening surface. When I tested it with a finger I understood why. It was glossy and hard as glass. Even as I looked, a fly alighted and, believe me, so far from sticking it couldn't even get a foothold on the slippery surface. It skidded sideways and fell off, the most surprised fly I'd ever seen.

I destroyed my handiwork furtively before Monica should see, and my only reminder of the fiasco is my best paintbrush, which is still set so hard it can be used as a hammer. Plus an unhappy conviction that old Caveman Armstrong wouldn't live long in the jungle if life there is on the flypaper standard—and more especially if spongebags don't count.

CHAPTER EIGHT

AFTER LONG PERIODS with a mere couple of days or so at home every fortnight, a real seven-day-leave was always an Event. Indeed, it used to take on something of the nature of a return from school for the holidays. Metaphorically I used to bounce out of the Air Ministry door swinging my satchel and grabbing caps off Wing Commanders' heads.

Particularly enjoyable always was leave in spring, when the change from town life to country life seemed most marked. For you leave the desk in the artificially lit room,[1] you leave the Air Ministry, that hive of gloomy passages, musty files, conscientious but uninspired Clerical Officers, young lady Temporary Clerks, for ever apparently boiling tea kettles on gas rings; you leave the scurrying crowds of Aldwych and the echoing station platform; you leave the dreary bomb-pocked outskirts of London, and all at once you are among the little gardens of Suburbia. Foaming with laburnum, lilac, pear and cherry, gay with rock-plant, wallflower or tulip, you can scarcely believe that little over half an hour previously all you had of spring was the exiguous green of the trees lining the pavements of Kingsway. You even for once find yourself envying the daily-breaders and eight-thirty-catchers who go back to all this each evening.

The train rattles along and soon comes the first big station that can by no stretch of absorption or imagination be called part of London's suburbs, or even semi-detached dormitory. Why, it even has an "announcer" of its own—just like big sisters Waterloo or Victoria.

---

[1] My room, being down a well in the middle of the building, was steeped in perpetual gloom, and I had to have the electric light nearly all the year round. Its annual ration of sunlight was a patch on the window-sill half an hour either side of midday every June 21st.

These station announcers, by the way, are one extraordinarily good innovation that the war has brought into wide use. The old method of finding which train was yours was either (*a*) to ask somebody in the carriage before you got in—the person you actually asked, of course, never knew, but one of the others did (or occasionally thought she did, but also didn't); or (*b*) to ask a harried and rapidly-moving porter pushing luggage—getting a barely intelligible and rapidly receding answer. Then with the war the porters became fewer, moved more rapidly and spoke more unintelligibly, while the people in the carriage who didn't really know where the train was going, apart from their own destination, increased in numbers. About this time— luckily for all travellers—came the loud-speakers. One just waited and listened—and if you hadn't caught it the first time it was repeated within half a minute.

The voices, of course, were not exactly Joseph McLeod or Bruce Belfrage. They varied naturally with the part of the country where the station was. Dialect was prominent. I don't mean you got real Loamshire: "Heer be Little Woold'm and this be Old Willum a-talling 'ee 'bout trainses." But in Devon you got a good West Country burr and in Lancashire you got "Laancasherr, ba goom." The most striking announcer of all, I remember, was at Guildford where for some time they had a lady announcer with a voice that was so terrifically "refaned" that it sounded as though she was speaking a foreign language: "Geelfford! Geelfford! thees ees Geelfford! The treyne now stending at Pletform Twoo is for Godalming, Meelfoord, Witleh, Heyslemeah, Leephook, Lees. . . ." And so on. Shattering enough in ordinary conversation, but when shouted at a defenceless herd of passengers it amounts almost to mayhem. Other travellers on the Portsmouth line will, I'm sure, back me up. But at least it hypnotised one into rapt and profitable attention.

Another famous announcer was a man at a junction on

the Brighton line whose voice was so loud that it was reputed to have been heard on quiet nights for miles down the track. Passengers aiming to change at his junction used to go to sleep quite happily, knowing they wouldn't, indeed couldn't, sleep past "George." Then one day the Southern Railway transferred him temporarily to a station farther down the line. That night all the junction passengers slept confidently on till they heard his voice, woke up and bundled out happily —only to find as the train pushed off into the darkness that they'd missed their proper station and, in the case of those on the last train, were actually stranded for the night.

But I, too, seemed to have got stranded on my journey home on leave. . . .

Soon, as the train goes on, you are in country you know; you have changed from the fast train and are on the slow one, stopping at small two-porter-power stations, increasingly familiar. Finally there is your own. It now only remains to catch the bus out to your village, and that is easily done. In fact you can't miss it because the train service and the bus service work in very skilfully together. That is to say, their respective time-tables have been so arranged that the bus goes from the station every two hours and your train doesn't get in till a quarter of an hour after each bus has left. This gives you one and three-quarter hours to catch the next. Ample time—no rush at all!

Twenty minutes on the bus and you are at your stop— by the farm at the bottom end of the village. There you find —if holiday time—a convoy of children to escort you home, and there is the house and garden waiting. Three hours ago your feet were on pavements and the scenery was battered, shabby London: now you are on grass and your scenery is spring at its freshest.

Sling suitcase, hat, mackintosh and, in the early days, the never-to-be-worn gas-mask and steel helmet down, unbutton tunic and come round the garden.

Being spring, the rock-garden and the dry-stone wall are

a sight. Aubrietia figures largely, of course; the usual mauve is mixed with the deep purple of *Godstone* and the deep crimson of *Bonfire*; also all present and correct is the delicate pink variety called *Rosea splendens*, which gets darker as it grows. Growing in with the aubrietias are *Alyssum saxatile*, striking clumps of yellow-gold, and the massed white of the evergreen perennial candytuft *Iberis Snowflake*. This last— since it shows up the other colours—is most valuable in rock-gardens because the white Arabis is by now nearly over. Arabis comes out earlier than other rock-garden subjects, and though most welcome in the rôle of herald, has few other coloured things in bloom with it. I always thought it rather wasted because I'm not terribly keen on white flowers entirely by themselves. But then in 1937 I discovered that a pink Arabis, flowering of course at the same time, was just on the market—and I bought some plants of that from Messrs. Bakers of Wolverhampton. It was called *Arabis Aubrietioides*,[1] and now I have a pink as well as a white curtain-raiser to the pageant of the rock-garden proper.

Passing through the rock-garden on the top lawn, we round the corner under the old yew into the rose-garden. A mass of blue at once catches the eye at the far end of the rose pergola. It is a little three-tiered rockery, built of white stone, each tier being eighteen inches high and planted thick with *Muscari*, or grape-hyacinth. This three-decker architecture gives the impression of a wall of intensest blue framed by the perspective arches of the pergola.

Incidentally, I'd never seen my grape-hyacinths so good as on my first spring leave in 1941. I counted the blooms in a single square foot and made it sixty. Next year they weren't nearly so good; they had grown too thick and made more leaf than flower. Grape-hyacinths are extremely prolific, scores of little bulblets forming each year round mother bulb, and though they can be left severely alone,

[1] Sutton's also have one called *Delicate Pink*.

my own feeling is that it pays frequently to lift and replace with more elbow-room.

Grape-hyacinths, by the way, are a most useful flower for cutting, as they will last two weeks and more in water. They slowly fade from azure to lavender-grey but are still decorative. If you deliberately don't put them in water for an hour or so after cutting, and so let them become "droopy," you will find that the heads will pick up after their drink (just like you and me, brother!), resulting in a most attractive "S"-shaped curve to the stalk.

Continuing round the garden we find the tulips everywhere in full flaunt. Some years ago I took a sort of rough census and found we had got something like fifteen hundred blooms, not taking into consideration all those Monica had been steadily swiping to decorate the house. Well, fifteen hundred is a nice lot to look at, but when it comes to lifting after they've flowered, and earthing up in an out-of-the-way corner and then replanting in autumn, as the experts advise, it's far too many to tackle. I did it for the first two or three years after we had the cottage—and when we had far fewer bulbs—but eventually gave it up in favour of what seemed more important garden work. The main reason, of course, for lifting tulips at all is that they are unsightly in a bed while dying down and yet you mustn't cut off the top-hamper when green, or they tend to come up "blind" next year.

If you do lift and earth up your bulbs, by the way, remember to mark the spot carefully, or you may not find them five months later when all the tops have withered off. Even so, though you dig them up in the autumn as sedulously as a Wild West miner sifting through his pay-dust for nuggets, many of the little bulblets which have formed round the parent—"pups," as Friar calls them—get left in the ground, and grow to adolescence and maturity on their own. We still have occasional tulips coming up in a corner where I earthed up some bulbs as long ago as 1931.

Since, as I said, we now haven't time to lift all our tulips each year, we've taken to planting them very deep in the earth so that the ground can be forked over and other things planted without disturbing them. Tulips don't seem to mind how far down they are planted —though the correct depth is three to four inches—and can make their way up from incredible depths. On the other hand, they do not  at all like being too near the surface—apart from the risk of frost—and a tulip bulb that considers it is not deep enough and is getting desiccated by the sun will often actually send one thick root down from the bulb to the required depth and form another bulb at the end of it, with proper rootlets and all, while the old bulb gently transforms itself into a wayside station instead of a terminus.

Most of our tulips grow all mixed up, Early and Cottage and Darwin, exact varieties unknown. They are either the unnamed ingredients of a sort of *olla-podrida* I once bought in a small sack—at a bargain price, for it was late in the season and many of them were sprouting—or else they are the bulbs which were already growing in the original cottage garden.[1]

[1] One of these, particularly prolific, has a most striking red flower with white stripes (or else white with red stripes), somewhat reminiscent of half-eaten Brighton rock. It always catches the visitor's eye, and they always ask me its name and I have not the slightest idea and so my reputation goes down the drain. It *might* possibly be a Bybloem type, the variety *Calypso*. Anyone know?

Apart from these, we have some nine or ten good named varieties, invested in when we laid out the bigger garden. One of the most attractive of these, to my mind, is *John Ruskin*, which has a lovely effect of pastel shades, a sort of pale mauve-salmon and cream overlaid with apricot (the description would make a gourmet shudder); but *Panorama*, a mahogany bronze, runs it close and is particularly admired by Mrs. Friar. Another variety, *Pride of Inglescombe*, is rather a funny one, because it starts off white with a carmine edge to the very pointed petals; then the pink slowly spreads as the tulip grows, till the whole flower is blushing hard as if it were a shy young lady who has just been told a *risqué* story. For yellows we have *Mrs. Moon* and *Inglescomeb Yellow*; the former has long pointed petals, while the latter is almost round, rather like a canary-coloured ping-pong ball.

By way of showing how one can be too clever, I must confess that, although I had had those two yellow tulips for years, it was not until I was writing this chapter and refreshing my memory from a catalogue that I realised I had got the two mixed up. When I first got them (from Sutton's) I labelled them as per packet, but when *Mrs. Moon* came up with pointed petals, like *Pride of Inglescombe*, while *Inglescombe Yellow* came up fat and round, I assumed the peculiar petals were an hereditary trait of the Inglescombe stables and changed the labels round, in the self-satisfied belief that Sutton's had made a slip in the labelling. It was therefore not till eleven years later that it dawned on me I did not after all know as much about tulips as Messrs. Sutton. The pointed petals are a characteristic of a certain type of tulip, no matter where or by whom grown.

Carrying on with tulips on the strength at Margarets, we've also got *Dream*, a very tall mauve fellow; *Afterglow*, an orange-pink affair; and two good pinks—rather similar—*Princess Elizabeth* and *Clara Butt*, supposed to be the two best pink Darwins—or were at the time we bought them. And lastly we have *Orange King*, in a class by itself because of its delightful scent. It's funny how many people seem to be quite ignorant of the fact that a tulip can smell at all. As a matter of fact, several of them smell very beautifully; *Mrs. Moon*, for instance, is another. We grow *Orange King* in two fat rows by themselves in the "cutting border" specially for the house; and believe me on a warm day a bowl of them fills the room with a perfume that I can't possibly describe; it's very fresh and quite unrelated to any other flower scent that I can recall for the moment.

Wallflowers, of course, we also see everywhere as we go round the Unencumbered Fee Simple on our home-coming spring inspection. They are the mainstay of any spring garden, but I'll ignore them here, as in an earlier book I wrote at boring length about the varieties we have. My favourite, however, is *Eastern Queen*, which with the brown-pink buds and pale apricot flowers gives the bed the variegated colouring of an old wall of light brick.

Of the flowering shrubs the *Forsythia* is mostly over; the lilac only just beginning. The *Prunus Pissardii*, however, is a mass of copper leaves and delicate pink and white bloom. Also doing their stuff in no mean fashion are the Siberian Crab, the Japanese Cherry and the sweetly-scented *Viburnum Carlesii*. But the "show-piece" of our garden in early May is the fifty-foot-long hedge which curves round half the drive and separates it from the upper lawn. It is formed of *Berberis stenophylla*—I saw a clump one spring in Kew Gardens, which gave me the idea—and it is now an absolute solid wall of tiny golden bell-like blossom. The flowers are so vivid and so profuse that the general effect can only be compared to gorse in full bloom. Later on, when they start to drop, walking on that part of the drive is rather like strolling through Aladdin's cave; one is shuffling through pure gold dust.

I have never seen any other hedge made of this shrub, though of course there must be many in existence. On the other hand, it is not a tidy hedge at all, because it grows long, thin, arching shoots—often as much as two and three feet long in the year. It is delightfully described in Messrs. Hillier's catalogue as "of rather lax habit." (The old *roué!*) You *can* "tidy" it for the winter by chopping it close back in autumn, almost to yew-hedge neatness, but I don't advise it. Friar and I did it one year—and discovered that the shoots we had cut off were nearly all the ones which would have borne the blooms next spring.

The other half of our almost circular drive—which curves in from the road round a four-foot-high bank with daffodils and so to the garage which backs on the road—is hedged by *Ribes sanguineum*, the American flowering currant. This too is now in bloom, the tiny apple-green young leaves mixed in with the flowers which hang like gouts of blood. *Ribes* is a most welcome spring shrub; for, like *Cydonia japonica*, the flowers start before the leaves.

Some people don't like *Ribes* in or near the house because it smells strongly of "cat." I first encountered *Ribes* about twenty-five years ago when occupying one spring a ground-floor room with a window looking out on to a shrubbery. Another occupant of the house was an aged cat called "Tom," and I launched a vigorous series of daily complaints against him for mistaking my room, in no doubt absent-minded senility, for any one of the nice flower beds elsewhere. I could not accuse him, however, from visual evidence, only olfactory; and at length my amused host traced my suspicions to a *Ribes* in flower just outside the window!

It took a bit of living down, and the worst of it was that a few days later poor old Tom chose to die a lonely and un-discovered death in the same shrubbery. For days afterwards my further complaints were treated with contemptuous hilarity, until the corpse was discovered—in an attempt by my host to find out on my behalf which strange-scented shrub was guilty this time—and I was exonerated.

We have other kinds of *Ribes* in the garden, though not in a hedge. *Ribes albidum* is a white pink-tinted variety and very pretty; while *Ribes aureum*, the "Golden Currant" or "Buffalo Currant" is delightful. It flowers later than the other two with little golden flowers, very sweet-scented. It needs a lot of cutting back as it spreads wildly outwards year by year, sending up fresh stems from the roots—ever seeking *lebensraum*.

We have also a very interesting hybrid between this and the blood-red one, called *Ribes Gordonianum*. It has bronze-red flowers with coppery-yellow centres.

We seem so far to have neglected the vegetable garden in our spring tour. Come through the green door into the walled garden then, and here we . . . one moment, what do I see ? . . .

I'm afraid I'll have to leave. The first asparagus is up and ready for cutting. *This* is the best spring sight in the garden.

CHAPTER NINE

Now THAT we're halfway through this book, I rather feel the time has come to explain why it was that, though in the R.A.F., I seemed to be able to continue year after year in a soft job in the Air Ministry, with the chance of getting home regularly to my own house and garden—instead of having to leap into a Spitfire and shoot down two Me. 109's before breakfast.

Well, no one would have been more surprised than myself if I had been told that day in 1940 when I first started to work in the Air Ministry that five years later I should still be working in it. Quite frankly, I should have been horror-struck at the very suggestion. But it was true. I went to the lower end of Kingsway—already by then practically solidified Air Ministry, for standing at the Aldwych corner you couldn't throw a stone in any direction without hitting an Air Ministry building—and there I stayed for sixty-three months. I had an office; I had a desk; I had a job.

And what that job was I'd like to put on record—before I forget it myself. For though it was a writing job—mere trouser-seat polishing, and so hardly what you'd call intrepid birdman stuff—it was most interesting, indeed unique, and I was extremely lucky to have got it.

I say that I was lucky to have got it: in point of fact, there was a little more than luck in my actual selection. One might say it was really swift work on the part of my brother who, though in the Royal Engineers, was attached to the Air Ministry as a sort of Master of the Royal Air Force Maps. For when the idea of the job was first under discussion the R.A.F. officer who had been detailed to look for a suitable "body," happened to mention in the presence of my brother that the R.A.F. was in need of an author for a certain new venture. My brother promptly said that he knew of the very

chap and embarked on a forty-horse-power panegyric—
secure in the knowledge that the other was not aware of the
relationship. Impressed to the point of awe by this apparently unbiassed testimonial, the officer in question set the
Air Ministry strings vibrating forthwith; in a fever of
anxiety to secure this most eminently suitable paragon
without delay. The result was that within a week I was
asked up to London for an interview with Somebody Very
Senior.

The proposed job—for which I was to be made a
Squadron-Leader—turned out to be to create and run a
regular monthly publication on training matters for R.A.F.
air crews. It seemed that the boys weren't reading all the
valuable information that the Air Ministry was putting
out for their especial benefit; and as far as I could see, after
investigation, I couldn't blame them. For most of it seemed
to be written in turgid long-winded "Whitehallese"—six
words being used where one would do—besides being badly
presented in uninspiring pamphlets, choked with small print;
or even on Roneo'd sheets, frequently only semi-legible. Here,
for instance, is a perfect example from a booklet about how
and when to use oxygen. The writer, wanting to start with
something like "Here are some facts about oxygen which
pilots ought to know," actually began thus: "*In an endeavour to correct some misapprehensions which exist in the minds
of even the most experienced pilots in regard to oxygen, the
following short Memoranda epitomises some common facts about
oxygen.*"

Small wonder that lads who were busy flying, handling
complicated machinery, and daily risking their lives on
operations, hadn't time to give to it; and since it was after
all basically good and valuable stuff, they were missing a lot
of good gen[1] that would have helped them very considerably
in their job.

[1] Gen—in case any readers don't know—is the Air Force term for information of all kinds. The origin of the word is not clear. Some say it is an

Well, to resume, I came up to town and after my talk with the Somebody Very Senior, decided—with some misgiving, for I'd never been an Editor before—that I thought I could do what was wanted. I was told, therefore, to get cracking; in other words, make out my application for a commission, then go before the Selection Board for approval and finally be medically examined. All this I was told would be mere formality, as it had been agreed that I was taking the job on.

The medical examination certainly was a formality— once the doctor got the idea I was going to write and wasn't to be allowed to touch an aircraft under any circumstances: but when I went before the Selection Board with my application, the elderly President—who, I believe, was a retired officer in civilian clothes—failed to grasp the idea at all. He seemed to think I was trying to get in the R.A.F. under false pretences. I tried to explain that I'd already been selected by one of the Air Force Big White Chiefs for a writing job and that the Board had merely to put the official rubber stamp on it, but he only started to ask searching questions about my suitability for a commission. The fact that, as he could see from my papers, I'd held a Regular Army commission for ten years, plus a further fifteen on the Reserve, before being invalided out just prior to the war, didn't weigh with him. The King, it seemed, might not be particular about his Army, but the R.A.F. was evidently a very different matter.

Again the fact that my papers had been signed (as required) by two high-ranking officers, who had known me for many years and officially certified that I was honourable

abbreviation of "genuine information." But this I don't think is so, because the Service distinguishes between "pukka (or reliable) gen" and "duff gen," which is false. Squadron-Leader Ward-Jackson, in his small dictionary of Air Force slang, "*A Piece of Cake*," gives this as the definition, but adds that in his own opinion it comes from the fact that at one time official documents were marked "For General Information." My own theory is that it is somehow derived from the fact that on the R.A.F. Stations it is to the Intelli*gence* Officer that one ordinarily goes for the latest operational information. The 'Gence Officer who gives out the "gen."

and my statements therein were true, didn't count. He wasn't going to be swayed by that either—documents probably full of lies, by gad! He read every word with ill-concealed scepticism, and suddenly pounced. Peering at me across the table he said suspiciously, "I see you've put down your profession as 'author and playwright.' *Written any plays?*"

I replied meekly that, funnily enough, that was one of the reasons that had motivated me in calling myself a play-wright; whereupon he said: "Ha! What plays?"

I smiled triumphantly. *This* was where I had him. He was at last going to be put in his place and realise just who he was dealing with. For *Ten Minute Alibi*—with its two-and-a-quarter years' West End run, six tours and so on—was by way of being a well-known title. Indeed, at one time, the newspapers had pinned the phrase on to a certain prominent murder case. So I said with assumed modesty: "I've written several plays; but perhaps the best-known was called *Ten Minute Alibi.*" I then waited for "Collapse of elderly party, who had thought that, etc., etc."

But I was the one that was deflated. For with a puzzled look he turned to a colleague and said: "Ten Minute *what?*" Very salutary for me!

Anyway I just scraped past him, and was later told to get uniform and report at the Air Ministry in eight days time, as a Pilot Officer, destined after the official time lapse to be a Squadron-Leader—without, however, any Squadron to lead, in which decision the authorities couldn't have been more right.

I reported as ordered, was given an office and the part-time services of a young civilian clerk. I then said, "Well, what exactly am I to do?" They replied, somewhat uncon-ventionally: "We're waiting for you to tell us?" I realised with relief that I was being given a free hand. This certainly suited me; for in the Services, where there's so much rank knocking about, a certain tendency often develops amongst some types of senior officer to interfere in work which is outside their province, merely because the fellow who's doing it is junior. But the Air Force seemed O.K. in this respect. Not only had they gone outside the Service and got a professional author to do an author's job—instead of scraping up some stray officer temporarily doing nothing much, but who had once had a couple of articles in a paper and was therefore An Author—but having put, oddly enough, a square peg in a square hole, they actually left him to get on with it in his own way. It was, in fact, tacitly agreed that I wasn't going to teach senior officers how to fly, and they in return weren't going to teach me how to write. Full marks to the R.A.F.!

Well, to cut a long story short, I sat about and moved around and saw people and explored the amazing world of the Civil Servant—which I had never encountered before— and tried to think up ideas, and argued and cajoled and learned that a feather-bed could be just as much an obstruction as a brick wall—more so because you *can* break through the one but not through the apparent yieldingness of the other.

Finally, after studying all the other official publications there were, I evolved my own monthly magazine. The basic idea, as far as I was concerned, was that it was to be absolutely *different* from all existing Service productions in shape, cover, presentation and everything else—particularly in its writing, in that it would try to avoid Whitehallese like the plague. If, for instance, it wanted to say (the classic example) that some people "drink but don't get drunk," it would sternly resist the temptation to write that they "are strongly addicted to the consumption of alcoholic stimulants, but rarely, if ever, prolonged their potations to the stage at which complete intoxication supervenes." Instead, it would read, I hoped, much as a person talked. And above all, it would have a leavening of humour; both humorous interpolations and drawings. In fact, its very cover—a blue

one, not the usual official pale buff—bore the Air Force
Eagle, kindly drawn for me by Fougasse; but an eagle
wearing spectacles and reading up gen from a book!

After wondering for some while about a title for my new
baby—for the appellation "Training Memorandum" (which
is what it actually was) was enough to sink a battleship—I
found myself idly jotting down on my blotting paper, just to
see how it looked, the initials of "Training Memorandum,"
spelt in full—"Tee Emm." I little knew when I first did
that that the time would come when over thirty thousand
copies monthly of "Tee Emm" would be published in the
U.K. alone—with separate printings in Canada, Australia,
South Africa, Middle East and India—and that it would
become a household word in the Air Force.

All the stuff in "Tee Emm" was either written by me or,
in the majority of cases, written up by me from material
or articles on training subjects supplied by the Air Ministry
Training Department or by R.A.F. Stations. This re-
writing gave a certain homogeneity to the thing: it also
allowed me to insert humour and to conduct major operations on Whitehallese. In other words, "Tee Emm" was a
bus; the passengers were provided by the authorities; but
the bus conductor dressed them properly for the journey and
undertook that they would arrive at their destination—the
minds of the young pilots and other members of air crews.
"Tee Emm" guaranteed, that is, that what went into its
pages would be *read*: it put the jam of readability round the
powder of valuable information. Painless education, in
short. Our official motto was: "Take ' Tee Emm ' regularly
—prevents that thinking feeling."

In all this, of course, I had the valuable assistance of a
certain Pilot-Officer Percy Prune, who came into being for
our first issue and stayed with us till the end. The original
suggestion that we should have a regular "character" was
made by a friend, Wing-Commander L. H. ("Joe") Stewart.
I thought it a grand idea; and thereafter P.O. Prune *was*.

P.O. Prune was pictorially created—that memorable vacant face—by our staff artist, Corporal W. Hooper, now better known as "Raff"; his remarks and characterisation were provided by me. Indeed, Prune came to life in record time and in a short while was known to all the Air Force as the Service's affable dimwit. Fatuously exuberant yet permanently bone-headed, he invariably made a complete muck of everything he set out to do, and was an awful warning to to all potential bad or foolish fliers. "A good landing," says Prune, with a crashed and smoking aircraft in the background, "is one you can walk away from." It is perhaps not exaggerating to say—indeed many instructors and senior R.A.F. officers have definitely said it—that Prune, with his constant boobs and miraculous escapes from accidents due to his own folly did a very great deal towards helping to keep down the number of careless flying accidents and thus saving lives.

For a long time many people believed Prune actually existed; for I had provided him with a desk and chair in my office, plus his name on the door. Naturally he was rarely found in—but even more rarely found out. Within a year I had got his name and number (mine) in the Air Ministry telephone directory. (It may be there still: I hope so for old times' sake).[1] People used to ring him up and write to him and send him rude presents and come in to try and see him. My invariable answer to 'phone calls—

[1] Unfortunately it is not. I heard later that a few days after I had left the Air Ministry a Civil Servant had come round checking up telephone numbers in the changed offices. By then Prune had had considerable publicity (including even a "fourth leader" in *The Times*) as the R.A.F.'s fictitious character, and so the new tenant of my office, when asked about Prune's telephone number, merely laughed and said something about it having been a great joke. The Civil Servant, however, drew himself up, heavily scored Prune's name out of the directory and said: "He'd have been out long ago, if I'd known he didn't really exist."

Frankly I don't know whether to be angry or awed at the above. Angry at the total lack of any sense of fun displayed in refusing to keep the little jest going: or awed that after five years, to say nothing of all the newspaper references, there was still someone in the Air Ministry itself who thought Prune was a real person.

any time up to 6.30 p.m.—was, "Sorry, he's not back from lunch yet." Caught out once by an indignant female who said, "But it's not yet midday," I had to think quickly. "Not back yet from yesterday's lunch," I amended.

Though Prune had managed to get into the telephone directory—if you don't believe me here's the relevent extract—

Name and Rank		Room	Tele.
Proctor, W. C.,			
S/L. ..	W69a/III	5073	Tels. 2
Proper, J. B., Mr. ..	V306	289	D. of A.
Protheroe, C. V. C.,			
Mrs. ..	39	28	R.C.S.
Proud, E. B., S/L. ..	FS312	1573	O.F. 3
Proud, H. J. G. E.,			
A/Cdre.	FS607a	1156	S. & O.P. (P.W.)
Proud, J., Miss	T405	1648	Typing
Prous, S. K., F/L ..	Y107	4247	D.G. of E.
Provost Marshal	MT118	MT34*	—
Prowse, B. L., Mrs. ..	X602	3514	P. 4 (Cas.)
Prune, P., P/O. ..	P602	2403	Tee Emm
Pryce, N. L., Mrs. ..	JB100	JB23	Accts. 15 (d)
Pryce, W. G., F/L. ..	A341	2740	E. S. 6 (a)
Pryor, A. S., Mr. ..	D805	2767	F. 8
Pryor, J. M., Miss ..	C508	8672	Typing
Pryor, W. E., Mr. ..	PX60	PX133	Science 3
Pudney, D. H., Miss			
	W133/IV	5488	Tels. 4 (b)
Pudney, J. S., S/L.	W11/1V	5408	P.R. 3
Pugh, F. B., Miss	HN415	HN4	Accts. 2 (d)
Pugh, J., Miss ..	JB100	JB25	Accts. 15 (d)
Pugh, S. M., Miss	JB300	JB130	Accts. 15 (b)

he failed to make the grade for the Air Force List. I tried it on, but perhaps it was asking a little too much. My own idea was that the little line, "Prune, P.—commissioned 1/4/41," among the many thousands of Pilot Officers would surely be overlooked, and could even, if challenged, be explained as a typographical error. But the Civil Service branch responsible for the printing of the Air Force List would not Take the Responsibility of "making the misprint," even though I had had a chat with the very high-up-indeed Air Council Member in whose department that branch was, and who had intimated that he certainly would not Notice It Officially, and indeed thought it a grand joke. A pity, for once in the List Prune could never, being non-existent, have been either removed or promoted. It

would have been fine to see, say, in 1995, right at the top of
the pilot officers the name of an elderly and gallant P.O.
commissioned in 1941. But perhaps I was suspected of
aiming to draw his pay and allowances.

One big point in Prune's fictitious career was when in
1941 an "Efficiency Expert," conducting an investigation
into what every one actually did in the Ministry, saw
Prune's name on the door and asked me just what *his* job
was. At first I thought he was being funny; then realised
he just didn't know. So I gave him a synopsis of Prune's
duties. It was embodied in the official report to go up to
the Air Council, but alas! a Higher Clerical Officer of the
Civil Service, horrified at such subversive goings-on, gave
the game away.

On another occasion, this time in 1944, when our Commando and air-borne troops were being trained to use
initiative by being given unusual missions to carry out on
their own at short notice, my office was invaded by a couple
of sergeants. It seemed they'd been suddenly given the curt
assignment to get Pilot-Officer Prune's signature and report
back as soon as possible. They were at the time about two
hundred miles from London and had never even heard of
Prune, but it says a good deal for their resource that
though they had only set off the previous afternoon, here
they were in "Tee Emm" office.

The trouble, however, from my point of view was that
when I told him Prune did not exist, that he was just a joke,
ha, ha, they wouldn't believe me. There was his name on the
door; there was his desk: they might be only "brown jobs,"
but they hadn't come as far as this to be made fun of by a
wingless wonder in blue uniform. As they were large,
hefty types, I quickly changed my tune and said that as a
matter of fact P.O. Prune was really extremely busy in the
next office and couldn't be interviewed by anyone at all, but
if it was to help the war on I'd see what I could do for them.
Whereupon I went next door and returned with a paper

bearing the signature which I had some while ago evolved for answering Prune's correspondence. Whether they ever knew they'd been having their legs pulled or not, I don't know.

As a matter of fact, the Service had indeed taken Prune to its heart in a big way and certainly were using him to pull the legs of the unsophisticated. A naval officer, for instance, about to go on forty-eight hours' leave to Edinburgh from the South of England, turned up, complete with kit, at a near-by R.A.F. Station and explained that a friend in the Fleet Air Arm had told him that a certain P.O. Prune would be delighted to fly him there, as he loved doing long trips like that to improve his very ropey navigation. He was solemnly told that Prune unfortunately couldn't do it, as he was at the moment two days overdue on a flight from Croydon to Heston.

And again, about the end of 1941, some readers will remember that every Saturday night at the Grand Central Hotel, Belfast, there used to be a phone call for Pilot Officer Prune, who was solemnly paged all over the hotel. He never answered.

I had also invented, after about a year, the " Most Highly Derogatory Order of the Irremovable Finger," which was awarded every month for outstanding examples of stupidity by members of the Air Force. (Prune was, of course, the Patron of the Order.) We subsequently learned that the M.H.D.O.I.F. was taken up quite widely by many R.A.F. Stations. They would have a replica of the insignia—a plaque showing an index finger, *inflexant non-movant*[1]—made in the workshops and any wretched officer of the Squadron who "put up a bad black" would be condemned to wear it in the mess for a whole day to expiate his "prunery." It was a sort of dunce's cap on a more exalted plane. I often wonder to-day how long our little *jeu d'esprit* will continue in being in the Air Force.

[1] The reference, of course, is to the Air Force phrase, "Pull your finger out!" meaning roughly, "Get a move on and don't be a damn fool."

Well, "Tee Emm" jogged along happily month after month, run by a staff consisting of me, "Raff," W. Gordon Williams as Civilian Assistant Editor, and a succession of Civil Service clerks, each in turn known as "Enoch." (Later, in 1944, this set-up changed to a W.A.A.F. Assistant Editor— a charming red-headed Section Officer, at once christened "Copper"—and a Warrant Officer, one J. H. Lea. Plus, of course, "Raff."

Volume II succeeded Volume I, then III, then IV. By the end of March, 1945, there were forty-eight "Tee Emms" in existence—for naturally the first issue had appeared on April 1st, Prune's birthday. In awed surprise I found myself starting Volume V.

In September 1945 my Demob. Group suddenly came up, and I received a curt notice to take my bowler hat in a week's time. I told the authorities this and they said, "If you go ' Tee Emm ' will have to close down." Though flattering, this was in a way true, as I had not only created the paper but run it for the whole of its life, and time would be needed to find another Editor. The alternative, however, was for me to commit immediate infanticide. So I said I didn't mind staying on for a few months while they made up their minds about the magazine's future.

At the end of that time they said it had been decided that "Tee Emm" must after all cease on my departure, no other Editor being available. At this point I suddenly realised that there were now only three more issues needed to finish off the fifth volume. So I said that if they wished I'd stay that three months longer and round off the "Tee Emm Five Year Plan" with a neat bow of ribbon, as long as they didn't mind my running it from home and only coming up to the Ministry when absolutely necessary. To this they kindly agreed, saying that provided "Tee Emm" was on time and in the same style they didn't care what I did or where I worked.

This pleasant arrangement, in fact, led to "Tee Emm"

keeping up to the end its reputation in the Air Ministry of being, at the most charitable estimate, slightly loony. For working, as I then was, principally at home and only visiting London about once a week, I naturally had not bothered about taking any leave. Then all at once I realised, with only about ten days in the Service still to go, that leave, though now purely an academic proposition in my case, at least carried with it a free travel warrant.

There was just time, and I put hastily in for a seven days

leave. The fact that it coincided with my final squaring up at the office when I actually had to be up at the Air Ministry for a week on end for the first time for three months, was not really my fault. But it considerably worried a lot of my friends there who, voicing sarcastic surprise at my appearing in my office for a whole stretch of seven days at a time, were gravely informed by me that I was *on leave*. Indeed I had —quite truthfully—put down on my leave form in the column for *Address While on Leave*, "Air Ministry, Kingsway." The general feeling after this effort seemed to be a pious hope that "Tee Emm" would close down and get the hell out of it before they *all* went nuts.

Thus on April 1st I finally pushed off, leaving behind

me, as a tombstone, five full volumes of somewhat unconventional official journalism. Indeed, in our final farewell number I actually started writing a serial story, leaving it "to be continued;" but no more "Tee Emms" to continue it in. I often wonder how that serial really does end.

But enough of London and "Tee Emm" and the Air Ministry. Let's get back to the garden, the house, and the family.

CHAPTER TEN

THE LONGER one lives in a settled routine the quicker time seems to pass. Yet invariably you are quite surprised at the realisation. A man will trudge hour on hour along a road, till suddenly he happens to look back, and seeing the passed milestones and the changed scenery he says, "Gosh, have I really come all that way in such a short time?" On the other hand, constant variation of environment and frequent changes of habitat—this sounds rather like an ornithologist talking about the Lesser Blue-rumped Cornswoggler—often leave in your mind the impression that what was in point of fact but a few weeks has actually been a couple of large æons.

As an example of this last, I remember, about seven years before the war, going on a trip with a friend. He had leave from the army and the idea was we'd expand our minds by visiting Scandinavia in a big way. So we planned out an itinerary to cover as much as possible in the time at our disposal, for we intended to go places rather than stay places. And we certainly did.

We went—if you'll excuse a paragraph or so of reminiscent maundering—from London via Newcastle to Bergen in Norway and had a couple of days there, where needless to say it lived up to its reputation and rained all the time. Indeed, in Bergen the horses are said to shy if they meet any one not carrying an umbrella. We then trained to Voss, motored across mountains to a place called Ulvik, where we stayed a day and night and rowed on the famous Hardanger Fiord, feeling very Viking; thence we moved on by steamer all down the long Sör Fiord via Odda to Breifon. Here we spent the night and next day motored right up over the plateau to Dalen. From Dalen we went off by steamer again, but this time along a canal only which at some places had

a series of locks like a staircase, to Skien and thence to Oslo
by train.

A couple of days in Oslo, then to Stockholm for three
days, during one of which we went over to Finland and back
—by night steamer across the Gulf of Bothnia—to a place
called Abo (pronounced apparently "Oboe," and also called
Turku, to make it more difficult.) We went there simply
because we thought the name funny and wanted to see if
it really existed.

After Stockholm we journeyed by motor coach diagonally

. M. D. A. :

down Sweden, spending a night en route at Motala on the
edge of Lake Vattern, almost an inland sea, to arrive at
Gothenburg for the night. Thence across the ferry, past
Elsinore, for a couple of days in Copenhagen, then night
train to Hamburg—due for a pasting in ten years' time
such as few cities would get—and after a day and night
there, finally back by Transatlantic liner to Southampton.

We arrived back feeling as though we had been on a
world tour. I at least had a vague feeling I'd find the two
children quite grown up and myself probably a grandfather.
Yet in all we'd been away just two and a half weeks!

But—resuming, rather breathlessly, at the point where I started to digress—when you are living a routine life, such as mine was at the Air Ministry, with the more or less regular fortnightly forty-eight hours at East Downing and the occasional seven days' leave, time, I found, simply leapt onward without my suspecting. Particularly had this been so in the case of the children: they too had been simply leaping upward without my knowing it. I was, however, shocked into realisation of the fact by discovering one day a "Nursery Register" I had made out in the first months of the war. I had been inspired to this by the whole family receiving its Identity Cards and my having had at once to explain the idea to ENHM.40.3 (vide her registration card) aged seven years old. When she further asked why "Old Teddy" (E. Bear, Esq.), doyen of the nursery toy-cupboard, hadn't got a card too, I realised that the authorities had been guilty of a grievous oversight, and so in a light-hearted moment I lined up the toy-cupboard personnel and made out the Nursery Register, or Census, referred to.

What, however, gave me the shock on seeing it again in 1944 was that I automatically assumed for some time that Felicity had been ENHM.40.3. But no, the seven-year-old was Toni. Felicity was ENHM.40.4 and had been only three at the time. And now Felicity, in 1944, was eight and a half, actually a full year older than Toni had been when the war started and the Nursery Register was made. Those war years had certainly flashed past.

I spent a happy but nostalgic half-hour rereading that Nursery Register. It recalled to me many old-time toy-cupboard personalities, men and women of consequence in the nursery of those long-ago days.

There was, for instance, the aforementioned "Old Teddy." Well do I remember him. Increasingly bald, stout, going grey in patches, and lacking an eye, result of a heroic defence of his womenfolk and dependants against a marauding kitten. He was also chromatic round the muzzle, owing to

his habit of being given portions of ENHM.40.3's food when
ENHM.40.2 (Monica) was out of the room. Remembering
the kitten, no doubt, he was invariably stripped for action
down to a pair of knitted red woollen pants. He was popularly
supposed to be wedded to Doll (always pronounced Dorl)—
at least they faced each other across the breakfast-table every
morning, and if that isn't a binding tie, what is? He, I saw,
was described on the register as: *Male. Birthday: Dec. 25th,
1930. Married. Occupation: A.R.B. (Always Ready for
Battle) and Nursery Warden.*"

The next entry was "Rose." Rose, I recollected, was
always a great favourite, in that she used to occupy the only
doll's pram nearly all day. Then one day she had to go up
to town for an operation at Hamley's Hospital and came
back quite changed. Her disability had been a serious one,
resulting from answering back Sally, the bull-terrier, and
when two females fight . . . Well, half her face had gone
and one eye was right inside her head, where it rattled
gruesomely, and she had lost all her hair from the shock.
It was later found in the dog's basket, and for some while
played the part of Leading Paleface Scalp in Red Indian
games. But when she came back we were all shocked. For
she was rouging much more blatantly; the oculist's work
had resulted in a wicked glad-eye that didn't quite shut, as
before, when she lay down; and, worst of all, she'd gone
peroxide blonde. That, it seemed, was what London did
for a girl. So Rose had been entered up on the Register as:
*Female. Birthday: Dec. 25th, 1936. Single. Occupation:
Glamour Girl or Worse.*

Then we had "New Teddy." He naturally hadn't the
years of his patriarchal namesake. Nor was he so grey:
indeed his hair was very thick and very deep brown. He
had a tendency to overdress, invariably wearing woollen
pants, coat, cap, muffler, bootees, a feeder at meals, and what
looked like the remains of a perpetual heavy jag, owing to
his habit of letting his head slump forward. By day-time he

would sit for hours on the landing; at night-time he occupied ENHM.40.3's bed, still fully dressed down to his boots and with pyjamas on over the lot. Registered as: *Male. Birthday: Dec. 25th, 1935. Single. Occupation: Heavy Sitter.*

After him came "Blue Teddy." We seemed to run to Teddies in those days. He was only about six inches high, and, I recollect, appeared one birthday morning in bed alongside New Teddy's cot. From the strong family resemblance he was obvious some relation, probably a New Little Brother. But whereas New Teddy was ultra-brunette, Blue Teddie was ultra-marine—though this might have been due to cold. For, in contrast to his elder brother, Blue Teddy never wore any clothes at all, not even a feeder at meal times. Entered as : *Male. Birthday: Jan. 27th, 1936. Single. Occupation: Under School Age.*

Next on the list was "Dorl." She was definitely half-witted. She had a completely flat nose of the same pancake prominence as her inane painted grin and indeed all her features; and at times the sawdust used to run out of her boots. How Old Teddy, her husband, put up with it each morning across the coffee cups we never knew. Dorl's one accomplishment was acrobatics: she could do the splits or lift an unbending leg straight up behind her neck, but it was all rather indelicate, as she was never really dressed for it. *Female. Birthday: unknown. Married. Occupation: Unpaid Domestic Duties.*

Then came "Golly" (coloured). He had of course the usual Aframerican penchant for flamboyant dress. He spent most nights, as I remember, between the door and the jamb of ENHM.40.4's bedroom, keeping it ajar in case she cried. It gave him a pronounced waist-line, but we suspected he was proud of it. He spoke with a Harlem accent and always needed a haircut. *Male. Birthday: Jan. 27th, 1937. Single* (there was a strong nursery colour-bar). *Occupation: Bedroom Doorman.*

Next, "Muriel." From her habit of standing simultane-

ously on her forehead and her toes, we were always well aware that she was excessively proud of showing off her very sketchy undergarments. She used at one time to be more modest, but I'm afraid Rose—after her London jaunt —had had a bad influence on her. *Female. Birthday: Feb. 23rd, 1937. Single* (so far, but Soldier was always a fool for a glimpse of undies). *Occupation: Contortionist and Exhibitionist.*

After her was "Blue-Bunny." He was life-size, but coloured azure and white in halves. He suffered from prolapsed left ear. He once took a solitary jaunt in a neighbouring field where he ensured a whole week's scared sobriety for a local farm-hand who'd stayed too long at the local. *Male. Birthday: Feb. 23rd, 1938. Single. Occupation: Temperance Reformer.*

Then we come to "Bimbo." He led at times, as far as I
remember, a wraith-like existence, in that he depended upon
air for his contours and couldn't always hold on to what
he'd got. In appearance he was bright yellow, and something of a cross between Disney's Pluto and a Lion Passant
Regardant. Or in his less flatulent moments, a Lion Passant
Floppant. His hobby was swimming, diving, etc., at bath-
time. *Male. Birthday: Aug. 21st, 1939. Single. Occupation:
Unpaid Aquatic Duties.*

Finally we had "Soldier." He was in daily charge of
Bimbo, but did not bathe. A very smart gentleman in a
red tunic with pipe-clayed equipment, and would have been
even smarter if he hadn't at one time in his career been
debagged. Some low tavern brawl, we feared, in an out-of-
bounds area, for the missing garment never turned up. As
he hadn't a spare pair, and no under-pants, his loss of
dignity and soldierly bearing was somewhat marked.
Registered as: *Male. Birthday: Dec. 25, 1937. Single* (but is
Walking Out with Muriel and very remarkable they look
together, too—for there's no doubt at all, even to the casual
passer-by, who wears the trousers in that ménage). *Occupation: Bimbo-Watcher.*

Ah, well, it all comes back to me—what possible interest
it is to you I can't imagine, but it's too late now—though I
found it hard to believe that the small seven-year-old daughter
who inspired that Register is now a typical school-girl with
letters home in complete character—full of "Thanks piles
for the tuck; it was super. Being a border is simperly
luverly. I think I was nearly sick yesterday."

Her best effort, by the way, which I still have, was a
sudden request to me to write a play which her form could
act at some half-term "do." It ran: "Please could you write
a short play lasting for about twenty minutes and sixteen
people in it please, the costumes must be quite simple, the
parts easy, and can it be very funny indeed. Thanks piles if
you can, but don't bother if you are to busy. If it comes off

I'll probably be in it, seeing your writing it." Even though I don't hold with dramatists squeezing their girl-friends into their plays, I should have been annoyed if Toni *hadn't* been given one of the sixteen parts I duly provided. For after all, there were only seventeen kids in the form.

And as for Jomfrey, who was a schoolboy of twelve and a half at the beginning of the war, in 1944 he was over sixteen, stood nearly six foot two in his socks[1] and weighed as much as I did. A solemn but shattering reminder of how long I'd "been in."

From my point of view Jomfrey's size had certain advantages, for by the end of 1943 he had grown out of my treasured, and no longer obtainable, gardening gum-boots and I was allowed to have them for my own once more—not to mention other articles of clothing. But there soon turned out to be a rift in the ointment, if not a fly in the lute. This was clothing coupons. The boy had grown so fast that coupons were for him about as long-lived as confetti—even the extra ones for "outsizes" to which he was entitled. Whereupon Monica ganged up on me on his behalf. I was in uniform ninety per cent of the time, she said, and when home merely worked in the garden where I could wear my old clothes; so I certainly didn't need coupons for civilian purposes. And as for uniform, she said, I had started out with two complete outfits of hard-wearing material which wouldn't need replacing for years. And as for underclothes, she said, in answer to faint protests from me, they didn't show anyway and wasn't she prepared to darn socks, pants and vests to the last inch of original material? Who was I, in fact, she said, to need coupons at all? Why, I merely collected the generously-filled Service books as they came along and sat on them like a miser on his unspent gold.

And so coupons were wrested from me, both uniform ones

[1] Still apparently unconscious of his height, he wrote home about this time describing a new master as "a very big man of about six foot."

and "specials" which were for "sports kit if required."
Monica was quite unscrupulous in using them too. If told by
an over-conscientious shop in our local town of Midfield
that she could not present my book, she'd select what she
wanted, step round the corner to the post office, cut out the
required number and post them to the shop then and there,
which after all was in accordance with the regulations.
Indeed I wouldn't have put it beyond her to purchase on my
book a Gresham's School cricket blazer, or even a twelve-
year-old girl's summer frock, and unblushingly represent it
as "sports kit urgently required by a Squadron Leader."

But perhaps the most Machiavellian effort was the
manner in which she made me buy new grey flannel trousers
to garden in because my own were getting, she said, so
indecent that the only garden they were now fit for was a
monastery garden.

With that attack the campaign opened. I, who love my old,
old clothes, held out for a while, but was at last reluctantly
forced to agree that perhaps I did need new trousers. I
explained, however, that I couldn't waste one of my precious
days of leave in going by bus into Midfield to get them, but
I'd do it when opportunity arose. She countered by suggesting I did it in London; and I countered by agreeing—and
regularly forgetting.

Then finally one evening as I was just going back to
London she said: "Be sure and get those trousers this time!"
I replied that I'd do it *next* time; on this occasion I had
barely time to catch the bus, and I didn't know the size.
This was of course routine avoiding action on my part.

This time, however, she fooled me. "I saw your best pair
upstairs on the landing," she said. "I'll run upstairs and
call the size to you out of the window." And she duly did,
skilfully catching me before I got to the garden gate.

About twelve days later, just as I was starting back home
on a forty-eight, I suddenly realised I had done nothing
about the trousers, and now had no excuse. I dashed into

a shop and said I wanted a pair of cheap grey flannel trousers for gardening. "Don't bother to run the tape round," I went on. "I have the exact size."

Having told him the size, he produced a pair, cut out my six coupons, took my twenty-five bob and suggested I might care to try them on. I refused, saying I hadn't time. Actually, it was a small shop with few facilities, and nothing to my mind is so embarrassing as to be caught dressed as the complete R.A.F. officer from cap to middle and thereafter continuing in grey flannel bags, or even in a pair of short and much-darned underpants.

"It was only to check the size, sir," he explained.

"Look here," I said. "My wife took the size from another pair of mine and if I, her husband, don't dispute her word, where do you come in?"

He saw the point—he was married himself no doubt, —and off I went.

Full of self-righteousness I displayed them that evening and next morning I put them on. They seemed a little funny. I called Monica and asked her advice.

"Why, they don't fit you at all," she said.

"But they're supposed to be the same as my others. Why, you yourself took the size and gave it me!"

"That's quite right. They were on a chair on the landing and . . ." A look of enormous contrition suddenly took possession of her face. "Oh, darling, I *am* so sorry," she said. "I *thought* that pair was yours, but I'm afraid I must have muddled them up with a pair of Jomfrey's and taken his size instead." Then, with the happy little smile of one who sees an easy solution, she went on: "But never mind. It's quite simple. He can have *these*, and you can get another pair when you go up again. It doesn't matter after all."

"Oh, not a bit," I said, staggered at the woman's duplicity. For there was I, twenty-five bob and six coupons down and still with trousers to get. And she swears to this day it was quite an accident.

CHAPTER ELEVEN

WHEN ONE AUTUMN I got seven days' leave—skilfully extended by brazen chicanery into eleven—I was welcomed with open arms by Friar. He reckoned there was "plenty's to do" in the garden; and it looked as if I was in for a hard spell. Not that I minded. Late autumn is always a grand time for the real work of clearing up the garden and getting ready for next spring. One feels rather like a scene-shifter, striking the third act, while the public are surging and seeping out of the auditorium on the far side of the curtain, and then setting Act I all ready for the next night's performance. (Dramatists, of course, often write plays in which the last act is the same as the first and so need not be struck after the show; unfortunately Nature never does.)

The chief job, of course, in the vegetable garden at any rate, was digging; getting the ground ready for rain and wind and Mus' Jack Frost to do their stuff during the winter months and so prepare the soil for new occupants.

A certain amount of ground was naturally still tenanted. Knobby-legged brussels sprouts were standing in warty rows; there were the neat lines of young spring cabbage; purple-sprouting broccoli and savoy cabbage also had their allotted quarters. But the ground where the peas and broad beans and tomatoes and sweet-corn had stood, and the beds from which the onion and carrots and potatoes had been lifted and stored all had to be prepared for next year's customers. And not the same customers either. As you know, some crops, like cabbage, cauliflower and brussels, take a lot out of the soil and these should not follow one another two years running. Potatoes, however—and roots like carrot, turnip, beet, and parsnip—can succeed any of these cabbage-type vegetables, known to expert gardeners as "brassicas"—and to Friar the only time he ventured on the word as something like "brassières."

Certain vegetables, indeed, seem to do particularly well after certain others. Here—from our own experience and not necessarily gardening Gospel—are a few hints in this direction. Runner beans flourish well when following potatoes; peas and broad beans in general thrive after the other root crops, carrots, parsnips and the like—and after potatoes too; the potatoes themselves can go back again on your pea and bean ground; onions grow well where your previous year's celery was, and so do early peas; and cabbages get on famously, in turn, in an old onion bed. . . . Isn't this about where we came in?

So much for the vegetables. In the flower garden, amongst a million other jobs, there were the herbaceous borders. They, I regret to say, hadn't been properly attended to for two or three years. Throughout the passing summers they'd been gradually acquiring That Middle-Aged Spread. The plants had been looking more and more bedraggled, the blooms fewer and further between, and the dead patches and general "morning-after" effect more marked. They needed lifting, thinning, digging, manuring and every other kind of beauty treatment.

Of course, if I'd been at home more and had had the time I would have been keeping a regular eye on things all along, but naturally the war years ruled that out as far as I was concerned; while Friar had all he could do to keep the veg. front intact. And after all, at Margarets we had nearly a dozen different herbaceous borders, of an average nine-foot depth, making a total of 215 yards' length in all—I've just been outside and stepped it!

However, I had nine days this particular autumn and no excuse for not tackling the job—which meant cutting it all down, seeing what gaps there were to be filled and which of the stronger plants, such as Rudbeckia, Pyrethrum, Michaelmas Daisy, Golden Rod, Iris, *Lychnis chalcedonica*,

and *Campanula persicifolia*, had got too big for their boots and would have to be reduced. When doing this last, by the way, it's a mistake, though it is certainly the easy way out, to chop all round the clump and leave the centre: for the best bits of most sturdy-growing perennials, like roast beef, are on the outside. You should lift the whole clump and replant a selected and preferably outside bit.

Once a border is cleared you can generally discover plenty of seedlings—one advantage of not dead-heading your plants too religiously during the summer. (That is if you want them. If you don't for Heaven's sake be ruthless; treat them as weeds and dig them up.) The silvery-leafed crimson-flowered Agrostemma or Rose Campion—*Lychnis coronaria* is its proper name—is always obliging: so are *Iberis*, the perennial candytuft, Aquilegia, and *Linum perenne*, the perennial blue flax.

The next thing to be done is digging and forking up between all the plants, so as to get the bed well open for the winds and rain and frosts of winter. After this you should try not to have to walk on it again—but generally you find there's something that necessitates it, such being the cussedness of life.

If you haven't been able, when your borders are clear, to dig in manure, it's a good thing to give them a dressing of fertiliser—not that I had time that particular autumn. A very good all-purposes mixture is bone-meal and potassium sulphate in a four-to-one proportion. It is cheaper than most prepared fertilisers, and doesn't hurt the plants if it gets on them. Choose a still day to put it on: otherwise it blows about and gets on your clothes and hair; and, bone-meal being what it is, you'll smell like a bit of main-drain for hours afterwards. So far from not even your best friends telling you why, quite casual acquaintances will harp on it very pointedly.

When the stuff is on, at about 4 oz. per square yard, it should be lightly forked in. I remember one pre-war year forgetting—or being too lazy—to do this for a day or so and nearly lost all the fertiliser off one border in an unforeseen manner. We had at the time four bull-terrier pups—or rather Sally, their mother, was at any rate a bull-terrier—and they were let out for their usual daily run on the lawn. They naturally, however, winded the bone-meal at once—any dog who couldn't ought to have an operation on his nose—and made a bee-line for the nearest border, where it was still lying white along the surface. I have never seen anything quite like the way they lapped it up. They simply ran back and forth, scooping off the top of the bed, soil and all, like an express train taking up water at speed.

It was some while before Monica and I and Friar could catch them in their excited manna-from-heaven mood, and by the time we did there were dozens of little muzzle-wide swathes of dark earth showing through the white. It was for all the world as though the demonstrator of an electric sweeper had been doing his stuff on a carpet specially sprinkled with flour.

Besides the herbaceous borders, the beds where you're going to sow annuals should be dug over too. Late autumn also is a grand time for transplanting shrubs and so on: the ground is wet, the earth has not lost all the stored-up heat of summer, and the frosts haven't yet come. You can move quite big things, too, without much risk of losing them, but if you know you're going to have to shift small trees and shrubs the following autumn, it's a good plan in the spring to cut deep down into the earth all round with a sharp spade two feet or so out from the stem. This operation cuts all the thick long roots and forces the tree to devote its summer growing season to establishing small fibrous roots nearer in. Thus you have a good central ball of root when you come to lift it, and the chances of losing it are reduced to a minimum.

I was told this, by the way, by a nurseryman. He said

each spring he did it with the subjects he expected to sell, or which had already been actually ordered for autumn delivery. The roots then "massed up" and were more likely to move well later on. He added that the extra labour was well worth it, because though it was his customers who replanted and cared for the trees, it was he who was invariably blamed for supplying poor stuff and asked to replace if they died from subsequent bad handling.

One way or the other in the last few years we've had to do quite a bit of moving of shrubs. The reason is that we bought most of our present flowering shrubs some while ago, at the time we were turning Margaret Cottage into Margarets. Naturally we wanted a lot of them; so for economy's sake we bought small specimens. Equally naturally, therefore, being pretty inexperienced, I put them in far too close together. Believe me, it takes a strong-minded and far-sighted man to plant very small trees the distance apart they ought to be when he's twelve years older, let alone the distance apart they really ought to be when he's a grandfather. If—under expert advice or pressure— you have forced yourself to do this, they look for the first three or four years too forlorn and pathetic for words. On cold winter nights you keep thinking of the poor tiny things shivering out there in their isolation instead of huddling together for warmth; while in the day-time unenlightened visitors are apt to ask sarcastically where are all the others; have the slugs eaten them?

No, the only thing to do in order to get your shrubbery planted on a proper long-term basis is to use your imagination and be hard-hearted. Try putting in stakes where you first think you want your shrubs; then find out their average ultimate size from a catalogue, stand back a little and endeavour to imagine each of them full grown. If you can do this, almost certainly you'll at once move your stakes farther away from each other. And while you *are* visualising them full grown, go indoors and do a bit of visualising

from any overlooking window where you have a view or
need light, to see whether they'll ultimately block that.
Probably you'll move some of your stakes once more.

The pruning of our flowering shrubs was another job
I tackled—in part at any rate—on that autumn leave. In
point of fact, for many of them it was the wrong time to
do it, but as they'd mostly been neglected by then for some
four or five years, I felt I had to have a go. Lack of proper
pruning makes them very top-heavy, which in turn means
tying and propping up if you don't want breakages in gales.

The pruning of flowering shrubs—if you really want to
keep the emphasis on the "flowering" rather than on the
"shrub"—is actually an all-the-year-round job. For some of
them flower in spring on old wood, i.e. wood made the
previous year; and some flower in early and midsummer on
old wood; and some flower in mid and late summer on
new wood, i.e. wood made earlier that same year; and all
have to be pruned differently and at different times, and
you have to know how and when. Personally long ago—
as I mentioned in an earlier book—I made myself a "Pruning
Calendar." In this I had worked out from catalogues and
gardening tomes exactly when each of the various flowering
shrubs which I owned had to be pruned, and how; and then
I wrote them down in chronological order of the months—
early, mid, or late. Thus at any moment I could pick the
list up and see what had to be done then and there. During
the war, of course, nearly all this went by the board.

Another thing, too, which needs frequent attention, and
which, therefore, my London job prevented being done, was
the *training* of the shrubs, i.e. persuading them to grow just
how and where you want them. I refer particularly to those
that grow round the house. With that constant attention,
i.e. tying up young and impressionable branches just where
they're in demand, or pruning some off so that the strength
goes into others which are already headed in the right
direction, you can make things like Ceanothus, Forsythia,

Cydonia japonica, and even the rampantly confused and enthusiastic varieties of Clematis, practically eat out of the hand. In the old peace-time days I used to walk round about twice a week snipping off a branchlet there or pushing another down under a corner of weather-tile there, with the result that they never had time to grow stout and intractable. This bi-weekly shrub inspection takes very little time and is well worth it.

It was on one of my quite recent autumn leaves that I first tried putting *Forsythia suspensa* up against the house, having previously only grown it as a bush in the shrubbery. Rather an untidy bush too, but one can forgive it a lot for those masses of flaming yellow in early spring. Nor need the gold be only out in the garden; for the way to prune Forsythia is to cut back the branches which have just flowered and give the young shoots which will flower next year a chance to make good. This means that, since they've got to go anyway, you can cut a lot of them when actually coming into flower and so have them in the house at a time when there isn't much to make an indoors show. As a matter of fact you *can* cut Forsythia long before the buds look like opening: keep it indoors in water in the dark, and you'll have it out in bloom well ahead of the parent bush in the garden—February or even late Janaury.

The two Forsythias I put up against the house I planted not far from the old Virginia Creeper—or rather, I should more correctly say, the ampelopsis—on the side of the original cottage part. Virginia creeper and ampelopsis, by the way, are frequently confused. Both are of the *Vitis*, or Vine, family, and both are often referred to as "Virginia creepers." But the true Virginia creeper is *Vitis quinquefolia* and it is the one which half-climbs and half-droops, if you get what I mean. If it doesn't secure the proper sort of support for its tendrils to help it climb, it will bend over and hang downwards with almost a weeping-willow effect. It has, too, large "five-fingered" pinnate leaves, whereas the ampelopsis (*Vitis incon-stans Veitchii* to pals) has a smaller leaf something like a maple and also suckers at the end of its tendrils, which means that it climbs and clings tenaciously, particularly on brick.

This, of course, was my reason for putting the Forsythia next it. I wanted to use the established and adhesive landlord in possession to train up the new non-supporting tenants. For I only had to pull a short middle section of reasonably thick ampe-lopsis away from the brickwork and push the Forsythia branches through the gap underneath. Thus they were held close to the wall without any trouble at all, and as an old ampelopsis has masses of interlacing strands all over the place, I could find a suitably placed one practically anywhere I wanted the Forsythia to go without bothering with tying it up.

For when it comes to proper tying you are nearly always involved in getting nails into walls, and if your house is at all well built it's a problem. (If it's a jerry-built bungalow, of course, a couple of strokes will drive a nail in so far that you can probably use the other end of it to hang a drawing-room picture on.) You are too wise, of course, to try to drive your nail straight into the solid brick, but you select a likely-looking crack, preferably just between brick and mortar, and start. The nail goes in a quarter of an inch fairly firmly and then it comes up against what feels like a sheet of steel. You hammer harder and harder and one of two things happens. Either the nail which you thought already fairly firm simply falls out of the hole as you lift the hammer for another stroke; or else there is a *zong* as you strike it and it suddenly flashes past your ear like a spent bullet. Don't bother to look for it. The rule is that a nail dropped in a garden is rarely found; or if it is, it will have a bent point and be no more use.

Occasionally after several wasted nails and much probing for a soft spot, as the war communiques say, you have luck and get one well and truly in. Then it's advisable to make use of stretched wires between nails to tie intervening branches to, rather than try to get nails in everywhere you want them. Wires on the side of the house may look a little unsightly at first but will soon be covered up, and the labour saved in nail-hammering is enormous, to say nothing of crushed thumbs, lost nails, lost tempers, and so on.

You'll find, by the way, that galvanised nails are the best for getting into brickwork, as they do not seem to bend or blunt so easily. An extremely good nail is specially made for this sort of work by a firm called Snow (at least Snow is the name on it). It is really a small four-sided galvanised spike and has a lead tongue going out at right angles to the top. Once the nail is in, this tongue can be curved over the shoot you are training and holds it there close to the nail as long as you like. It doesn't rub like wire does, nor eventually rot away like twine, while the great advantage is that at any time you want you can bend up the tongue and release the branch in a flash. For this reason it's rather a waste to use them on permanencies. They are more for things like *Clematis Jackmanii*, which have to be cut down each year to within a foot or so of the ground, in January or February, and then the new fast-growing shoots trained up again in the spring.

By far the best way, of course, of getting nails into a wall is to have them built in as the wall is being made, but then that's rather like Leacock's oft-quoted advice on how to make an asparagus bed—"dig a hole three-foot deep three years ago." We never thought of it for our house walls, but we did for the wall round the vegetable garden. We bought dozens of little four-inch-long galvanised tangs with eyelets in them and the bricklayer set them in the mortar at about four feet apart along every fifth row of bricks. Wires were later easily strung through them and all our fan-trained fruit trees—peach, pear, cherry and plum—are now tied in position to the wires.

I only had time for one other job that autumn leave and that was to help store the dahlias; for the night frosts had already come, and Friar had a few days before cut down all the blackened top-hamper and was anxious to get the roots under shelter.

The begonias, more delicate, had already vanished. When they go, they *go*: they collapse on themselves like pricked balloons. Our few tubers were already in a bag in the attic, which seems to suit them; and there throughout the winter they muse among themselves on their vanished glory. Rather like old actresses long past a job: "My *dears*, you should have seen me in the summer border. Day after day I knocked 'em cold. I can hear the applause still!"

The dahlias, however, are different: too many and too heavy to get up to the attic, and anyway we now have a better place for them, though at first it offered a problem.

The main idea, of course, is to keep frost and wet from the fat vulnerable roots, and the experts advise packing them in sand in a box and storing it in either a dry attic or a cellar. This we religiously set out to do the first year that we actually "grew dahlias." (Not *many* dahlias. All we had was the "Whatyoumaycallit Nursery's Special Collection of Six Selected Cactus Dahlias, Suitable for Beginners!") We dried the roots, packed them carefully in sand, and decided

I

on the attic. Well, that idea just stopped there. . . . Have you ever tried to carry a largeish box full of sand up to an attic? A mathematical friend told me afterwards that a box of sand only 18 inches square by 18 inches deep would weigh getting on for three and a half hundredweight, and ours was far bigger.

So we left it just where we'd filled it—in the tool-shed outside—and during the winter the dahlia roots caught something or other from the damp and changed into pulp.

Next year (with another "Whatyoumaycallit Special Collection") we tried a very little sand only and a shelf in the coal-cellar. This time the tubers got overheated and when we took them out they looked for all the world like shrivelled-up bits of string.

The following year we had another shot: needless to say with yet a third "Whatyoumaycallit Collection"—we were nothing if not triers! This time we solved the problem. We packed them in a box of wood-ash—which we got from the big log-fire in the drawing-room and generally reserved for the rose-bed, and which is far lighter than sand—and we stored the box, covered with sacks, *outside* the house but in the covered-in recess where the well and electric pump are housed. The natural warmth of the house is held to a certain extent in the recess and never lets it get too far below freezing-point even on the coldest days. And this, it seemed, was just right for the treasured "Whatyoumaycallits."

We also now have—thanks to a generous friend, which is the way to make your garden grow—a large number of a Dwarf Bedding Dahlia called "Lady Aileen," but we deal with these in a different way. The first year we had them growing here and there in the borders, but decided the following spring, when we replanted them after their hibernation, that we would put them in one long low hedge alongside a small curving grass path. They are about a foot and a half high and would, we thought, be most effective. They were; but next year we found that several overlooked bits of root had also come up perfectly unharmed in the old positions. So now we solve *their* problem by leaving the majority of them in the ground all winter, with a little extra earth or cinders heaped over them and possibly some litter, such as old fern fronds, as well. We lose a few occasionally, but it's well worth the saved trouble.

But beware of doing this with dahlias you particularly treasure, which may not be quite so hardy as "Lady Aileen." We tried it on with some of our cactus dahlias—in reality to save the labour of digging up and storing—and it didn't work. There was an extra cold winter that year, and as Friar said, "that put paid to they."

CHAPTER TWELVE

THE GARDEN, the house, and the family were by no means the only things that had to be kept going during the war. There was also the family livestock. This was largely ornamental rather than useful, ranging from Sally, the doyenne, via the cats and rabbits, right down to the latest addition brought in from the highways and byways, which might be anything from hedgehog to field-mouse or even a clutch of tadpoles.

On the more commercial side of the animal kingdom there were of course the eight or nine hens, as in nearly every self-respecting family with a bit of ground big enough for egg production; but in the early days of the war we had also kept half a dozen ducks. The idea behind this was a businesslike one: ducks laid larger eggs and laid them more often, every day in fact. And they didn't need a large duck-pond, as you might think. So long as you had the right sort of duck, Indian Runners, all they required in their run was a bowl of water big enough to wash their hands and faces and clean their teeth.

As a change from hens I found our ducks most amusing to watch. They invariably went everywhere in a sort of tight posse, as though held together by an invisible elastic band. Should one break away at all it was only for a very short distance and increasingly reluctantly—as the elastic stretched—till all at once it seemed to realise it couldn't keep it up any longer and snapped abruptly back into the group. At intervals, too, they would suddenly, as if at a signal, start loudly discussing affairs of state, but this habit proved rather wearing. For no one duck could ever make a remark without the other five simultaneously chiming in with their versions, and it is apparently an axiom that three ducks make as much noise as six, and six ducks sound like twenty-four

At first they did their stuff magnificently—every day, every duck, one large egg. Indeed if one of them was a little late in laying, the others stood round the outside of the duck-house and hurried her up at the top of their voices. Then for some reason they all took a dislike to the duck-house—maybe the plumbing went wrong—and started to lay all over their enclosure. As this was in the "meadow" part of the garden, where the grass was fairly long, it made egg-collecting rather a business. Entering to do so was rather like crossing an enemy mine-field, and often we only found the eggs by treading on them, which is a poor way indeed. What was needed of course was a sort of egg-detector, like the Sappers use for land-mines, but before we could enter into negotiations about this the ducks, as usual with one accord, stopped laying.

And when I say stopped, they definitely stopped. One always seems to get an occasional hen's egg or so—even when your birds go off laying—but these ducks just stopped dead and stayed that way. As they continued, however, to eat an enormous amount twice daily, it ceased to be a paying proposition. So after formally warning them that if they did not mend their ways they'd have to be remustered as table-birds, we carried out our threat and stopped keeping ducks—after a brief period of keeping fewer and fewer ducks.

So much for our excursion into duck-owning.

In 1944, by way of augmenting the larder, both our own and the nation's, we thought we'd take up rabbit-keeping in a small way. Friar and I went into partnership over this, owning the rabbits jointly. It was a true combination of capital and labour, for I bought two does and a buck, paid for material for hutches, provided the food and allowed them to be kept on my ground, while Friar made the hutches and was responsible for looking after them and feeding them daily. All profits, whether from sale in market, or to the butcher, or to friends wanting rabbits themselves, or even to our own kitchen for the table, were then divided equally.

Those first three rabbits, the destined progenitors of the Armstrong Rabbitry, we bought, I remember, from a Savage Club friend, one Tommy Lowe, then on the *Daily Mail* as Military Correspondent, who was an expert rabbit-keeper. (I should explain that he had a largeish place in East Sussex: he didn't keep them either in the Savage Club or the *Daily Mail* offices.) They came to us already named: Bebe Daniels, Sarah Churchill and—no, not Ben Lyon, whom Tommy wanted to keep, nor even Vic Oliver—but, rather unexpectedly, Sam Small of "moosket-dropping" fame. They were Rex Sables by breed, with lovely smooth dark fur, conjuring up gorgeous visions of motoring gloves.

Each doe had her first litter fairly soon—as rabbits will—but we were a little startled to observe that Bebe—though, as I said, both she and the buck were quite dark—produced two pure white ones in the bunch. This startled us: we didn't know quite what it meant. And when she did it again in her next litter we began to think that these two white blobs among seven or eight black ones were perhaps, like firing different-coloured Verey lights, some sort of signal. In short, was she trying to tell us something? We consulted Tommy, however, and he said it was just a kind of throw-back, that she was quite normal, and that we were not to worry. It might even be high spirits or wishful thinking . . .

So we gave up worrying, and as after that she only produced normally-coloured ones, we assumed that she'd given up sending code-messages or S.O.S.s and had settled down happily. And at least we got 19s. for one pair of whites, sold on the hoof in Midfield weekly auction market.

We didn't really find rabbit-breeding much of a success. For one thing we weren't on a big enough scale. Friar, however, seemed quite happy about it. But then he did not have the business of transporting them down to the butcher, or, unless we took him along specially, into Midfield market on Wednesday in the car—which also meant transferring them safely from the travelling boxes into the auction

market cages. And safely it had to be. Have you ever tried
to catch a loose, scared rabbit in a crowded market place,
especially when it's a real Market Place—*i.e.* the central
square of a busy little market town, crowded at the time
with cows, sheep, pigs, calves and so on and surrounded by
several shops, a church, two banks, three pubs, and a post
office, in none of which places is a loose, scared rabbit a
welcome customer? Believe me, as the Air Force say, there's
no future in it. Make up your mind right at the start and
write that rabbit off. Refuse to own it, or even know it.
It's wiser, safer and cheaper.

Another snag to commercial rabbit-breeding—even on
our small scale—is provided by one's family. The moment
a litter arrived, each daughter had to claim one for her own,
give it some absurd name like Wednesday or Toothpick and
thereafter take such a personal interest in the thing that
when the time came for it to go the way of all rabbit flesh,
we had emotional crises in the home at the rate of one an
hour for days beforehand.

And it was no good giving them the darn rabbit for their
own, and then washing one's hands of the whole affair.
They'd been tried out at keeping their own pet rabbit before
and had been found wanting. It simply meant that the
rabbits were loose in the garden half the time—"I was only
holding Fourpence in my arms and stroking him, Mummie,
when he jumped down and ran away"; or else some new
passion temporarily sidetracked the unfortunate bun, who
then had to be kept from starvation by Friar making long
journeys to the inaccessible parts of the garden where the
pet rabbits were parked, instead of being able to do them
en bloc. And on top of it all Monica suddenly produced a
rooted aversion to eating animals we had brought up—
coupon-free or not.

Soon, therefore, our interest in rabbit-keeping dwindled
and died—except when Friar at intervals produced bunches
of young rabbits to be taken into market and at intervals we

shared out the proceeds. It had just been a thing that seemed worth trying at the time.

The major portion of the Margarets' menagerie, as I said, was, however, purely ornamental rather than useful. There was Sally—and for a short while, though this was a year before the war, there had been the four pups I mentioned in the previous chapter. They were called Punch, Judy, Truda, and Winks. We sold two of them at pure-bred white bull-terrier prices; and subsequently had to refund most of the money, when it turned out that—as the would-be conjurer once brilliantly explained when he found he had smashed up the real gold watch: "I say, something—er— seems to have gone wrong somewhere." For all four pups were growing up into mastiff size and patches of black were also rather pointedly giving the lie to the pure-bred white theory. There had certainly, in spite of our care, been a technical hitch. The remaining two pups we gave to Pat Murphy of *Daily Mail* fame, who visited us one day, as mascots for his Sussex farm. He renamed them for some unearthly reason China and Gloup and reported six months later that they were still growing and had started tearing barn doors off their hinges with their teeth. We felt we were well out of it.

Next in importance after Sally came Tabs, Felicity's own special cat—that most favoured animal for whom nothing was too good. Food was brought to him; chairs were reserved for him; playthings were devised for him. (One of the latter incidentally was a live grasshopper—and I have never in my life seen a more surprised cat.) Even Friar gave him bean-mice which had been caught in the toolshed. On one famous occasion, Jomfrey thought that he'd try and add a bit of zest to a meal of dead mouse by pretending it was a meal of live mouse—much as a pseudo-French chef in a seaside hotel pours some office paste over a piece of boiled cod and calls it *Suprême de Morue à la Seaview Pension*.

So he tied a piece of string to the mouse and started

hauling it around the garden path. Tabs instantly was all worked up and pursued it with vigour, till he happened to stand on the string and the mouse promptly "died" in mid-flight. He sulked, had to be re-wooed and finally caught it. Jomfrey who was watching out to see that he bit the head off—because that was the part that had the string round it and a tummyful of string wasn't on his diet-sheet—was, however, caught napping. For though Tabs duly bit the head off, that was also the portion he immediately ate first, and it had, to his disgusted surprise, to be yanked back just as he imagined he had begun to digest it.

Later on, we acquired another cat. This was the result of a direct promise to Jomfrey by my brother's wife, who owned a lovely female ginger cat, which, as usual, kept having kittens. The father, by the way, who lived a few houses off and was also ginger, was not, like most tom cats, of the "love 'em and leave 'em" type. He used to take quite an interest in his progeny's progress and visited them frequently at night—slipping in through the hopper window of my sister-in-law's kitchen to see how they were coming along with their lessons, table manners, and so forth. He was also not above being the paternal tyrant; for one wet night my brother and his wife were wakened by one hell of a row in the kitchen below—pots and pans falling, cats squalling, kittens bawling. It died down fairly soon, however, and they realised it was probably only father having occasion, during one of his brief inspections, to smarten his family up.

It was, however, a little more than that; for next morning my sister-in-law entered the kitchen and found the mother cat crouched watchfully on the uncomfortable ledge of the dresser, one kitten in a state of panic on the top shelf and the other equally scared on the window-sill. And in the box under the kitchen table, where they should have been, slumbered Father—who evidently after his visit had decided it was really too late and too wet to go home now and so had done a little real "head-of-the-family" stuff, turned them all out, and bagged the bed.

But I digress. . . . One of my sister-in-law's many small marmalade kittens was towards the end of the war presented to Jomfrey as promised. We had specified a male because of Tabs, feeling that a visit to the vet. would enable us to hold the balance in the home nicely between love and battle. The selection of the correct operational type of kitten we left to my sister-in-law, who is practically infallible in these matters.

In due course a small ginger scrap arrived, was named Squibs, adored frantically by all the humans, fled from in ignominious terror by Sally, and completely ignored by Tabs. Jomfrey shortly after went back to school, whence his first letter home was chiefly composed of instructions about Squibs being taken in to the Midfield vet. and properly attended to. (Surely no last-generation mother ever had letters like that from a son at school!)

In went Squibs next market day and . . . well, you can guess. My sister-in-law, I said, is practically infallible in these matters, but the accent this time is on the "practically." Poor Monica, who had for the last ten years been knowledgeably and expertly dealing with young kittens, rabbits and such, had a most humiliating time trying to explain to a disbelieving vet. that *she* had not made a mistake, but just had taken her sister-in-law's word. For after all, one doesn't look a gift horse in the mouth, so to speak.

Tabs, of course, was delighted when we told him. He began to stay very close to home, and his expression whenever he looked at us seemed to say, "That's real service, that is!"

But, as I intimated earlier, our real headache was Felicity's gleaning of so-called pets from the countryside round. I should say it was really Monica's headache, for I was naturally rarely at home long enough to get more than the backwash.

Apparently it began with a laudable attempt by Felicity's

school in the neighbouring village to inculcate "nature-study." As a result her daily walk home, escorted by Monica, who used to go to meet her, was a sort of wild-life expedition such as might have been organised by some needy Zoo.

Everything that flew, hopped or crept was hailed with yells of delight, captured and brought back; while boxes, jars, paper bags, and every other known form of unobtainable container were hourly demanded. Each, very natural, decease was a cause for tears; each escape a matter for howls of fury, followed by recrimination—" *You* left the lid open!" " *You* moved the box!" and so on.

And at bedtime would come a torrent of instructions about "my beetle," "my worm," or "Willie," who—believe it or not!—was "my pet wood-louse." The final straw came one day when Monica was ordered by Felicity, in bed with a cold, to go into the rose-garden and catch greenfly for a starving ladybird.

After that episode Monica decided that since Felicity's school had started the craze, it should take more of the responsibility. She therefore issued a ukase to Felicity that every morning all nature-study specimens were to be incarcerated together in a specially-issued box, regardless of their variety, diet, age, or sex, taken to school and left there to be admired, fed or neglected by the pupils, but *not* to come back. This left her to deal only with the daily intake from the return journey. But if she hadn't been firm, Monica felt the next thing would have been a request that she should sit up all night with a sick centipede.

Mice, of course, were understandable as pets. Hardly a child exists that at one time in its life hasn't either kept or wanted to keep white mice.[1] Being in the country where harvest mice and other types were readily obtainable, we frequently suffered from mouse-in-the-house in a big way.

[1] Felicity has two white mice—Timothy and Matilda—at the moment of writing. Or rather, since she has now just gone to boarding school, which at the last minute very rightly refused to have them, I should perhaps say that Monica has two white mice at the moment of writing.

Jomfrey, at fourteen, was rather to blame for this, because he was pretty hot on catching them in ricks, at threshing time, and so on, whereas *Les girls*, left to themselves, would have a lot of good clean hunting without too much in the way of result. Jomfrey, however, not only caught mice for them, but was so expert at it he was even able to carry out detailed instructions as to type and colour—much as an old-time slave-ship captain would be instructed by his owners to bring back a cargo of Fantee rather than Bonny niggers on his next trip.

I quote the following letter from Monica, sometime in spring, 1943, by way of showing what that woman had to put up with:

"I have endured a variety of tempests since you went away and have been severely over-moused. Jomfrey spent most of his last morning at home out on a mouse-hunt. Luckily he was specialising in browns and discarding all greys, so eventually he only returned with one captive." Felicity, apparently, I gathered reading on, was so disappointed at not getting any returns that the soft-hearted Monica actually went to the rick with her in the afternoon and herself caught a pair of modest greys. But Jomfrey by then had let his mouse escape and "spent the rest of the waning daylight re-catching it all over the nursery floor with the aid of a torch, and finally was persuaded to give up the hunt only on the drastic threat of no tea—it being then nearly six. He next bethought him of *our* scorned greys and, as a final gesture, installed them with civic pride in his empty mouse cage, with impressive instructions to Felicity and me on their upkeep. After which he went back to school and left us to it.

"Next day one mouse was thought to be sick and so due for attention from Felicity. Whereupon it bit her hand and she turned it loose in a fury. The other grey died yesterday and was entirely disposed of by a grateful Tabs. In the meantime I have been ruthlessly haunted by mouse number

one, the brown, who for several days could be met galloping all over the house—in my bedroom, in Felicity's room, in the spare room, on the landing and in and out of the kitchen. Tabs sat hopefully about—waiting, of all things, for *me* to catch it for him. But at last the haunting has ceased and I think it must have found a way out. Anyway, I am now de-moused."

And that was only one of many such experiences. On another occasion, this time when I was home on leave, two of Jomfrey's mice escaped at once. One took refuge in his bed and just as he had gone to sleep woke him by running over his face—not *my* idea of fun. It was caught after an exciting chase by three of us, during which it managed to get *under* the carpet and proceeded to whiz about all over the floor like an air bubble. It was no good ringing it round because the only way of getting it out then would have been by cutting a circle of carpet. Finally it was herded to an edge and captured.

The other was last seen in the neighbourhood of Jomfrey's wash-basin and we hoped it had got down the wastepipe and been drowned.

Well, it had got down the waste-pipe, but it had not been drowned. It had apparently discovered that the plumbing of the house was a ready-made mousehole system. The shattering result was that late that night, while Monica was clearing away the supper things and I was about to fill the kitchen sink preparatory to helping wash up, the mouse suddenly appeared *up through* the sink waste-pipe.

I gave a startled yelp—as who wouldn't?— at which the mouse vanished again, but when I called Monica and tried to explain that the missing mouse, last seen on the floor above, had just popped up through the kitchen sink, she gave me a peculiar look and said something about the newly-arrived cask of draught cyder I had been tapping before supper.

Luckily a moment later the mouse reappeared. This time it startled Monica, because it popped up through the wastepipe of the other half of the sink—a double one—and not through the one at which she was looking. She tried to catch it, whereupon it disappeared and came up in mine, the wastes being connected underneath. For some while it fooled us in this way—and we had a lot of "Over to you," and "Your bird, Sir George!" till we put the plug in one half and restricted its activities. Then waiting carefully till after a few reconnaissances it gathered courage enough to move away from its base, we were able to put the other plug in quickly and cut off its retreat.

But I'm glad it *did* make that reappearance: otherwise I should never have lived it down with Monica.

CHAPTER THIRTEEN

THE GARDEN was very lucky during the war. It escaped bombs and requisitioning; our "vackies," during the early months, were kind to it; it wasn't made into a battle training ground, or even a defence scheme; and our valuable Mr. Friar was above the age of calling up. All the usual hazards, in short, passed it by. But it had its own particular war ailment all right. And that was weeds.

For our garden at Margarets was neither an established one; we had been slowly making it ourselves out of ploughed field ever since 1933: nor was it a complete one; as I said earlier, there were several unfinished patches, left till inspiration came, such as that which had only recently been metamorphosed into the pond. This meant, first, that by no means all the original more virulent weeds had been eradicated, as might have been the case in a more or less established garden with years of tending behind it; and, secondly, that our fallow patches were always a potential source of weed supply to the rest of the garden around and needed constant watching. Otherwise they all too quickly turned into spearheads of a highly efficient underground resistance movement.

Friar and I had, therefore, always been engaged in a life and death struggle against weeds. It wasn't exactly a losing battle, but it wasn't a winning one. Friar by the week and myself by the afternoons—except for a day or so in town every fortnight—were just able to keep the enemy in check, both the local invaders and the left-overs from the making of the garden.

When, however, in 1940 my country and London periods became reversed, it began to make all the difference to the spread of the weeds. I don't flatter myself that I really did all that amount of work. It was just that weeds being what they are, that little bit less control each year of war resulted in their increasing by arithmetical progression. A corner infested with creeping thistle, or other perennial weeds, and not properly attended to one year is twice as strong and twice as large next year; the succeeding year it is *four* times. And as for those annual weeds that freely seed themselves, such as groundsel or speedwell . . . well, the proverb has it that "one year's seed means seven years' weed." If this is so, it looks as though after our five war years we must now expect two and a half thousand times the amount of weed we perforce were unable to hoe up in 1941.

Anyway the garden now in this spring of 1946 is in a terrible state. I'm told that everybody's is; but that's not much consolation. I know that, in the case of some weeds, say bindweed—known locally as "that durned ole lily"— other gardens cannot have as much as mine. Nature just couldn't have grown enough to supply any other garden on the same scale.

It would be interesting to compare opinions with other skilled weed-growers as to which weed they consider Public Enemy No. 1. My personal view is that bindweed, or con-volvulus, of which there are the smaller and the greater, both evil, wins in a canter. For bindweed roots run every-where at enormous speed in all directions and through everything. Owing to their tendency to "come to pieces in me 'and," they are at any time difficult to dig up in their entirety, certainly in a border where the stuff has permeated the roots of your herbaceous plants. But with us it is a particular problem because we have not much depth of top soil and under it is a softish, easily-fissured rock, called "malm rock," a kind of bastard chalk. And down into this, often two foot down, goes this horrible nightmare of a weed. Add to this the fact that not only do those snake-like roots break so easily, but that every small piece overlooked —even half an inch or less—will grow again, generally

K

from both ends at once, and you realise that bindweed is for us a Major Problem, if not a Life Work.

One thing that can be said about bindweed is that it doesn't appear to seed itself. Another thing is that, on its existing form, it doesn't need to.

I have found no really effective way of dealing with bindweed; not even of controlling it, let alone liquidating it. Weed-killer will not reach all the roots—if it did it would have killed the roots of everything else on the way—and it is equally difficult to apply it to the foliage, because the moment the stems get above ground they start winding round and round the nearest unsuspecting neighbour, like a cowardly foe advancing on you from behind a screen of women and children.

In any case the trouble with bindweed, as with most of the creeping-rooted perennial weeds, is that it's not much good using weed-killer, even if you are able to do so. It only kills off the top-hamper; and there's plenty more where that came from. In fact, dozens of little viper-heads are at that very instant only an inch or so below the surface, and will in a short while burst up into the light with all the added energy and diverted nourishment that had been feeding their dead brothers.

Of course the accepted method of destroying weeds of this type—provided you have time—is religiously to pull off every growth that appears above ground almost as soon as it makes its first bow. The idea is that no roots can go on living if they are forbidden access to the light and air from which they obtain and store up their life-force.

Basically this is sound. If you have, for instance, nettles —perennial stinging nettles—growing in a shrubbery or flower border, you can prove it. Start in spring when the first shoots are two or three inches long, and nip every single one off at ground level. Do this again at the end of a week with the newcomers and reinforcements. Do it the following week, and regularly every week; and by August you will find that the new nettles coming up are neither so numerous nor so strong, and that you will quite frequently be pulling out long lengths of yellow nettle root which have withered and died under the strain of trying to give life to an enormous family which has been continually massacred in infancy. Next year you *may* possibly have to initiate another campaign, but only a brief and minor one.

And thus you have defeated your nettles—*provided* you have had the time.[1]

In grass land the same result can be achieved by regular scything or clipping of nettle patches, but they take longer to eradicate by this method. For before you can scythe them

[1] I should in fairness add that I have not tried this personally; I got it out of a delightful little book I once read on the subject of weeds by Sir Charles Boys. Like me, he was obviously a real weedsman.

effectively, they have had to grow to a certain height and meanwhile the roots have already been strengthened with a certain amount of the nourishment they need. You may thus have to repeat the treatment for two or three years. This is no doubt the origin of the old saying: "To get rid of nettles, cut them three times a year for three years."

But with bindweed this procedure just doesn't seem to work. As I said, it needs time—and I just don't seem ever to have had sufficient time. Moreover, bindweed is subtle and widespread, and there are always some of the wicked up-thrusting stems that you miss—till they triumphantly appear at the very top of some thick clump of Michaelmas daisy, having been all the while defeating your supposed starvation blockade of the parent roots.

If any one can show me an infallible way of getting rid of "that durned ole lily," rampant in borders, shrubbery and hedge, he'll earn my undying gratitude.[1]

The creeping thistle is another Bad Type in the same class. It has long sinuous white roots which dodge about underground like a tube system, sending up tall and very prickly thistles at frequent intervals. It can, however, generally be tackled with ultimate success in the same way as nettles, i.e. by taking the time and trouble to pull them all up as they appear.

But Public Enemy No. 2—in our garden at any rate—is, I think, the speedwell, that little creeping weed with the lovely blue flower in spring. It turned up on a bank in a corner of the Estate some dozen years ago, and because it looked so pretty I left it. Two years later it had spread considerably, still, however, rather to my delight. But an old gardener, paying Friar a visit, noticed it and said, "Once you've got that stuff in your garden you'll never get rid of it." And as far as I can now see he was dead right.

Speedwell is only an annual and therefore relies on seeding itself to exist, but it does this pretty thoroughly and

---

[1] Or, if he prefers, a copy of this book.

somehow seems very resistant to hoeing. It is so small-rooted when young that the root stays in any little unbroken lump of earth, even though hoed back and forth, and quickly grows on down in its new position. It then starts to expand by creeping over the ground and forming patches matted above and matted below; for though shallow-rooted it is always rooting itself again and again as it covers the ground. When, therefore, it gets into old clumps of phlox and similar plants, it has, although it is more or less on the surface the whole time and not deep down among the roots, practically to be scraped out from between the plant stems strand by strand. This digging, hoeing, scraping, forking-up of every little rooted fragment is, however, the only thing to do, if you want to clear it and you must do it before the flowers seed and start new colonies. Even so it is almost impossible to get it out of grass lawns this way—and, worst of all, it smothers and kills the grass. A proper type of some good lawn dressing is the only real antidote. Yes, speedwell has certainly earned its high position on the list.

Before passing to Public Enemy No. 3 I'd better mention a well-known criminal which, thank Heaven, we haven't got. (About the only bad weed we haven't.) This is horse-radish, and many people give it top rank in the devilish weed hierarchy. My advice, based on others' experience is: however much you like horse-radish sauce, refuse to have even one tiny plant in your garden. Refuse even to have horse-radish in the house. For the roots have to be scraped, pieces are thrown away in the dust-bin and sooner or later a fragment gets into the garden—and grows. Not even the pinch-off-young treatment as for nettles is any good for horse-radish: in addition to which it sends up shoots from any depth and from any small piece. Once in, it's with you for keeps.

After consideration, I think our particular P.E. No. 3 is the good old dandelion. True, it doesn't spread underground, but that's about all. It has every other trick: the root is extremely difficult to get up in its entirety and any left will grow again; pieces an inch long will grow on their own account; and in addition it seeds itself far and wide. On the other hand it is, upon further consideration, easier to get rid of than speedwell—except when it has rooted itself in cinder paths, drive-edges, stone walls and so on, because it doesn't spread itself and can at least be dug out. A fork or spade well down to the side and out it comes, often with a root over fifteen inches long.

In a lawn, however, digging out cannot be done in quite such a devastating manner, and from my experience the following is the best method, at any rate for large single ones. It does not, of course, apply to groups of seedlings. With a sharp knife, or spade, make a cut in the turf out from the edge of the dandelion root to about four to six inches away. Make another, in the same line, out from the other side of the dandelion to the same distance. Then shove a fork deep into the lawn about nine inches from and parallel to the cuts. Lever up slowly: the cut will gape like a mouth, the dandelion in the centre, like a tooth. Waggling the fork a little, extract the tooth. It'll come out nearly always intact, and a stamp downwards on the turf will remove all traces. And once in the groove you can do it almost as quickly as I can write it.

If you want to use weed-killer on dandelions—particularly when you have massed patches of young ones—I've been told that the best stuff is our good old friend sulphate of ammonia. (This is really all that lawn-sand consists of, plus a touch of sulphate of iron and ordinary sand to make it easy to scatter.) The sulphate must be dry and powdery and should be scattered lightly over the dandelions.[1] The leaves then wither away and—but this is where I don't quite believe my informant—the poison goes on down and kills

---

[1] Your sulphate will probably have to be dried and crushed to powder specially before application, as it has a habit of absorbing any water in the atmosphere if stored for long.

the roots. That bit sounds to me all too simple. It works with plantains and daisies, but then their roots are short compared with those of dandelions: even baby dandelions, though possessing a root no thicker than a piece of string, seem to be fired from their earliest years with the desire to visit Australia by the most direct route.

The same fellow also told us that another dodge, for big dandelions and plantains, was to take a skewer, dip it in diluted sulphuric acid and jab the weed squarely in the solar plexus. This, if your aim is good, does kill the root.

I tried it one summer for a couple of afternoons, but it's a tedious business, and so in 1944 I treated myself to a present —a "Weed Eradicator" which works on much the same principle. This weapon, about the size of a short rolled umbrella, is hollow and tapers at the bottom to a socket from which projects a stout four-inch steel needle with a groove down the side. This needle is held outwards by a strong spring so that none of the weed-killer, with which you fill the thing—via a cap at the top—can normally escape. The drill for weed-eradicating with this tool is to put the point of the needle vertically in the centre of the dandelion and stab downwards. The needle goes down the centre of the root, the resistance at the same time compressing the spring so that the top end of the needle is partly forced upwards into the hollow container, whereupon a gout of weed-killer is at once enabled to run down the groove and so into the heart of the weed.

As wielded by me, it wasn't 100 per cent. effective. Possibly I was too quick and didn't allow enough time for the liquid to run right down. Anyway the frequent result was that only the top died and, being a dandelion, within a week four more heads had come up from the living part lower down.

Another difficulty, I found, was to ensure getting the needle truly down the root and not to one side of it, the exact centre of a very leafy dandelion being often hard to hit off. But this I got over by taking a knife and just slicing off the top hamper. The cut root was then exposed as a white circle—a bull's-eye no one could miss. It took a little more time, but ensured accuracy, and you can save constant changing back and forth between sword and spear, so to speak, by doing a couple of dozen or so weeds with the sword and then going round them with the spear. To avoid over-looking any, you should of course leave the cut-off head close by to mark the scene of the crime.

Next on my weed black-list comes, I think, groundsel, largely because it is so prolific and so ubiquitous and seems to go on flowering and seeding quite happily in winter. Hoeing or hand-pulling is the only treatment for groundsel, but you must do this when it's young. Once it's started to flower, the plants, even though hoed up and thrown on a rubbish heap, will spend their last strength on forming seed. And the thistle-downy seed, when formed, doesn't stay put: it travels like an insurance agent. In fact, the mere act of hoeing is often responsible for distributing groundsel seed not only far and wide, but farther and wider.

Talking of groundsel, if you ever see in the spring little smoky-black-and-crimson winged moths fluttering labori-ously around don't kill them. Some gardeners are only too apt to kill any butterfly or moth they see; they are going on the principle—taught them by cabbage-white butterfly experience—that their caterpillars are harmful.[1] But this particular moth is the cinnabar moth and, if allowed to live, her black-and-yellow banded caterpillars will later appear—and they eat groundsel avidly, but not other things. Except, of course, ragwort (which is of the same family), but you shouldn't have that in your garden. Up on the Downs here where ragwort flourishes in large patches, I

---

[1] A tip about cabbage-white butterflies, while we're on the subject. It has not yet been verified by me, though I'm trying it this summer. It's based on the fact that you never find caterpillars eating rhubarb. Boil several rhubarb leaves and keep the water handy in the tool-shed for watering your cabbages now and then. The butterflies won't go near them after that.

have often seen plant after plant swarming with these caterpillars which will eat two-foot-high branching ragworts
down to a chewed six-inch stem in no time. And the turf
all round will be covered with travellers who have at last
left the tough bits of gristle on the side of their plates and
are searching hungrily for new plants.

Sow-thistle is in much the same class as groundsel. (At
least the annual one is. There is also a creeping one which
very soon takes possession of any neglected bed unless you
go after it with fork and determination). Charlock, too, is
very bad if it establishes itself, because the hard-shelled seeds
have a habit of lying dormant for years. But it has this
advantage: it gives itself away badly. Like mustard, you
can spot the bright yellow flower from a mile off, and it
comes up easily.

Daisies are bad things—particularly in a lawn, but
powdered sulphate of ammonia dusted over the leaves will
go far to settling their hash. The powder should be dry and
so should the weather. Sulphate of ammonia can also be
used with varying effect on many other weeds—plantain,
buttercup, hawkweed and, as I said earlier, dandelions.

Though I haven't space to deal with them individually,
I'd like to put on record that all the above mentioned are by
no means the full total of weeds in our garden. The following have also arrived and are in part possession—though
some of them I do not know by sight and have only our
visiting experts' word for it: knapweed, clover, chickweed,
yarrow, coltsfoot, pimpernel, toad-flax, hawkbit, hawks-
beard, goatsbeard, catsear and all points west.

In conclusion, weeds in drives, paths and other places
where you aren't at the same time trying to grow something
else, can be treated *en masse* with weed-killer. If you don't
like having arsenical weed-killers about the place, as perhaps
too much of a temptation to your wife in a moment of
provocation, you can use the non-poisonous types, or the
very efficacious chlorate of soda. Be sure you ask for, and

get, chlor*ate*, not chlor*ide*.   The latter is only common
or table salt.

Mix it up at the rate of two ounces or so to a gallon of
water, sprinkle lightly from a can and your weeds will
pack up.   One or two of the deeper rooted ones may try to
book a return date, but you can deal with them separately.

A word of real warning, though, about sodium chlorate.
It is one of the ingredients of fireworks, so don't water
anything else except the weeds.   If you were to dip a bit of
paper in a strong solution and then dry it off, it would
become so highly inflammable as practically to be explosive.
You should remember this if, say, you don't use up your
chlorate all at once and put the rest by till next year in a
paper or linen bag.   The salt slowly absorbs moisture from
the air, and by next year the bag will be impregnated with
it and when dried will be dangerous.   Don't try burning it
in the kitchen stove, for instance!   Though not actually in
the atomic class, it goes off somewhere between exploding
and burning.

For the same reason when watering your drive, if you
keep on wetting your clothes or boots you may in time
build up in them a good content of chlorate.   Just watch
this;   or perhaps when sitting peacefully one evening in
front of the fire with your feet on the fender, your boots
may blow up.   And don't say I didn't tell you!

CHAPTER FOURTEEN

CONTINUING for the moment with the subject of weeds—as though I hadn't said enough already, but gardeners, like hypochondriacs, love to talk about their ailments—I find I never mentioned couch- or running-grass. It's funny how in many of the learned treatises on weeds you'll often find grasses of all kinds omitted; yet when one "weeds" a flower-bed it is as a rule mostly grass you're dealing with.

Couch-grass is defined by the dictionary as "a widespread and troublesome weed." Indeed, it's one of the worst of all. (If you've read the last chapter, you will have gathered that they *all* are!) Like bindweed, small dogs, and urchins' noses it runs all over the place. Long brown snake-like roots with white spear-points twist and push all over the beds, sending up grass tufts here and there, but always pressing on to fresh fields of conquest. Unlike bindweed at any rate it doesn't bore down two foot or more into the rock, and so prevent extermination. Couch-grass generally keeps reasonably near the surface, and patient work, forking up and pulling out the long, stringy lengths, will dispose of it. That is, if during the process you don't mind disposing of a lot of other things too.

For every weed has one bad point. (Perhaps I should say that among every weed's many bad points there is always one outstandingly pernicious one.) In couch-grass this is an ineradicable habit, once it has got into a flower-bed, of making hastily for cover. And the cover it makes for is invariably the thick clumped roots of your best perennials. It will push straight ahead in the open spaces of the bed where it can be fairly easily dug up, without delaying at all, and merely sending up a few blades here and there to spy out the land. But once it reaches the safe shelter of Michael-

mas daisy, or phlox, or chrysanthemum or lychnis roots it
will twist and turn around on itself and settle in in a big
way, driving up large clumps of grass stems in the heart of
your flowers. It knows full well that if it is to be winkled
out of *that* strong-point you'll have to dig up the whole
well-established clump of whatever-it-is and then spend
fifteen minutes pulling the grass roots out of the flower
roots, as if you were unravelling a snarled skein of wool—
or getting the bones out of a grilled herring.

Another habit of couch-grass is the ability to travel miles
under brick paths or stones or concrete. You might think
that a broad path of bricks well cemented in would prove a
pretty good barrier to a mere bit of grass, that your flower-
bed on one side was well protected by it from any threat
of invasion from beyond the pale. But, no, the predatory
couch-grass battalions, studying the promised land from
afar, muster their platoons, go underground, and soon
reappear on the far side, fresh and fit and hardly out of
breath.[1]

An example of what couch-grass can do in this line was
the small circular bed I made round the Siberian Crab which
stood near the pond. As I mentioned in an earlier chapter,
when paving round the pond itself with my home-made
concrete slabs I had laid them also round this bed and
cemented them in. It was three foot wide, went all round the
bed without a break and, as I thought, more or less isolated
it. Once I had thoroughly cleared the bed of all perennial
weeds, it would be safe—except for wind-blown surface
intruders. As I thought! Within two or three months that
bed was a waving mass of couch-grass, which had converged
on it from all sides under the stones. With some labour I
lifted one of the slabs up to investigate. Like the club
committee-man who was asked whether a certain unpopular
candidate for membership had been black-balled or not and
replied: "Black-balled? Have you ever seen a plate of

[1] So incidentally does lily-of-the-valley. This sort of evens things out.

caviare?" all I can say to you is, "Running-grass under that stone? Have you ever seen a plate of sphagetti?"

Enough of couch! It's a painful subject.

Mention of the pond, by the way, reminds me that when I was busily discoursing earlier on the making of the paving round it, I omitted to say anything about the pond itself, which in point of fact was only finished some few months before I was summoned to the Air Ministry.

It was at first—before the paving and rockery came into being—just a pond, a lonely pond all by itself. But it definitely was a pond-in-being, an operational pond. The first water-lilies and other "aquatics" as the nurserymen say, had been planted in it; the first goldfish had swum in it. Incidentally the first toy boat had been launched on it, but that was strictly against the rules, because it was a lily-pond, not a dockyard, and I threatened that if I caught the kids throwing any more launching parties I'd be tempted to break something even more exhilarating than a bottle of champagne over them. . . . *Not* on their bows either!

And as if to set the final seal, the first person had already fallen into it. I regret to have to say that—to the vast amusement of the children—it was Daddy in person, on Christmas Day, when "testing the ice."

I'd thought about having a small pond for a long time before it was actually made, but only as an impracticable dream. For there was no water running through our garden, and moreover the ground was practically flat, so that it would have been difficult to collect water anyway. And the trouble about just making a pond, filling it, and then leaving it, is that the water becomes stagnant and in the summer evaporates very rapidly. Ponds, I had thus regretfully decided, were only for those lucky people with small streams or falling ground.

Then one day I was in the road just outside the Estate to the east of the drive gate. The road happens to be slightly sunken and a sloping grass bank runs up to the garden level some three foot above the road. It had rained heavily all morning and at one point about two foot down this bank a field-drain was discharging happily into the roadside ditch.

Field-drains, as you know—or as, like me till I came to live in the country, you don't know—are made of foot-long sections of earthenware pipe and run with the slope of the ground twelve inches or so below the surface. The sections being loose and uncemented, the water in the earth can soak into them at every joint and then, because there's less resistance to its flow inside the pipe than outside, it runs along till it discharges into some roadside ditch at a lower level. Flattish fields, inclined to be water-logged otherwise, are thus kept properly drained, and in good shape. Hours—even days—after heavy rain you may see in road banks these field-drain outlets pouring away like burst pipes, draining, with their subsidiaries, literally acres of field around.

Well, it was the field-drain just by my gate, busily splashing away into the ditch, which gave me the Big Idea. In its passage through my garden it ran quite close to the site I'd selected for my pond. I began to wonder if I could not somehow trap it at that point, make my pond for it to flow into and then pass the water through and out into the ditch at a higher level. Since it drained quite a few acres of ground there should be ample water to keep the pond well supplied.

After about ten minutes' thought I realised—what readers have probably realised already—that the field-drain at the site chosen was about two feet deep and that I could not raise the water in it to ground level merely by banking it up in a pond. Before I could do this, it would pile back in the drain, flow out at the joints and make a morass for some way back along its length. The surface level of my pond, therefore, would have to be the same as that of the land drain, two feet down, and then go down *further* for whatever depth I wanted it. This would sink the whole thing down into the bowels of the earth far too much : it would also mean far too much digging.

This woolly and stillborn idea, however, led me to my ultimate conception. And in case any one wants to know just how we did get a pond in a flat garden, this is what I eventually did. And it worked!

There were two notably wet patches in the garden about twenty yards or so away from where I wanted the pond to be—which was just to the east of the ribes hedge which bounded the drive. There was also, about fifteen yards or so away, a small wooden garage of the "Put-it-up-yourself-instructions-in-lid-of-box" type which I'd bought two years before to harbour Monica's small car.[1] The water from the garage roof, I decided, could be collected in gutters and led down into a small underground pipe: the water from the wet patches could also be tapped by short field-drains—thus killing two birds with one stone—and all three could be led into the pond, the necessary fall only needing to be ten inches or so. With the normal British rainfall the supply should be quite enough to keep any small pond reasonably full and freshened up, and the water level need not then be more than that ten inches below ground level. To make a two-foot deep pond below that would be quite a different proposition from *starting* at two foot down. And the pond overflow at the far end could be led through the bank into the road ditch at three foot down.

So on these lines we dug our pond. It was not a very big one. As stated earlier it was roughly the shape of a longish triangle—two long sides and one short—with one angle blunted off in a curve. The short side and round the blunt angle measured about eighteen feet, while the two longer sides were twenty-seven and twenty-four feet respectively. Where these two joined together at the sharp end was the outfall. These lines were not, of course, straight; they all had slight curves and bends here and there to make it informal. The depth was from nine inches at the broad end to fourteen inches in the middle and two foot at the

[1] Now *the* car!

deepest part just by the outfall. It was made of concrete four inches thick with a cement rendering over the inside. Just where the water came in was a little "trap" to prevent mud being carried in in solution—which seemed a silly thing to have done because later on I found myself ladling shovelsful of earth into the pond, when planting the lilies and other things I bought to grow in it.

It was a great day when the pond was at last finished and ready to hold water. Friar, I and Monica collected round, and I formally unblocked the in-flow from my special little land-drains and the pipe from the garage. All that was needed now was rain. Well, of course it didn't rain for a week—during which we waited impatiently, scanning the sky for any clouds the size of a man's pond. The hold-up began to worry me rather as I had already ordered the lilies and other plants, and the pond water had still to be purified.

This last is rather important and people who make ponds for the first time often forget, or don't know, about it, and then wonder why their plants die. The trouble, of course, is that cement contains lime, and fresh cement therefore is apt for some time to sweat some of this out and turn the water so alkaline that plants can't live in it.

There are roughly, I discovered, two ways of tackling this problem. The first is to paint the new cement over with one of the various commercial preparations—three or four coats are required—before filling it. The other is to fill the pond, then add permanganate of potash crystals till the water is wine-red, let it stand for three days, then empty and repeat. I haven't the vaguest idea which is the more effective. Doubtless they both achieve the same object, the only difference being that a permanganated pond probably looks down on one treated by the other method as rather a brazen painted-up hussy, while the painted pond refers contemptuously to ponds that have to look on the wine when it's red during two three-day binges before they're capable of doing their job.

Personally I adopted the permanganate method, even though it meant filling and emptying the pond twice. This indeed was rather a business; for as you'll have gathered, our pond had to be emptied by hand, i.e. by getting in in gum-boots and solemnly baling out with buckets. In a way, though, the permanganating was rather fun, for when you threw a handful of crystals in they sank to the bottom, leaving blood-red streaks behind them, which slowly spread across the pool in long waving streams like the condensation trails of a squadron of Flying Fortresses—or as my more

L

blood-thirsty eleven-year-old son remarked, "like a man overboard whose leg's been bitten off by a shark."

Well, at last all this was done just nicely before our plants arrived. Naturally our pond being of such half-pint size, there weren't many, but here's what we had, in case it's of interest to other intending pond-begetters. We got them from Hillier's of Winchester.

For the deep end, i.e. growing some eighteen to twenty-four inches below the surface, we had two lilies—*Nymphaea fulgens*, crimson, and *Nymphaea Laydekeri rosea*, pink. I did not want any white varieties, but *Nymphaea alba*, the native English water-lily, is a good one and easy to grow. I forgot about yellow ones till too late. Had I remembered, or had the room for it, I'd have had *Nymphaea Marliacea chromatella* (excuse these long names, but unless you get the names just right and go to a good firm, you won't get the right plant). *Chromatella* is a lovely water-lily, clear primrose colour with orange-gold stamens. The so-called English Yellow Water-lily isn't really a *Nymphaea*, but *Nuphar lutea* and its flowers look like little yellow tulips.

Also in deepish water, I had a thing called Pickerel Weed (or *Pontederia cordata*). This grows up to about two feet above water, with rather peculiar arrow-headed leaves and lavender-blue spikes of bloom. Called a weed, it spreads like one too, and later on threatened to dominate the pond. Bits of root would break off, float into water-lily territory and start growing there. I cut it round severely one year and then, while wondering what to do with this excess profit and not having the heart to throw it away, I suddenly remembered the man in Maurice Hewlett's book, *Rest Harrow*, who went round England secretly transplanting various rare wild-flowers from one district to another. So I carted great chunks of Pickerel Weed down to a stream about half a mile away and planted it there.[1]

---

[1] Whether it grew or not, I don't know: when next I remembered I'd done it and went down to the site to have a look, I'd forgotten just where the site was.

The fourth plant on our list was a Flowering Rush (*Butomus umbellatus*) which grows in anything up to one foot of water. It has rose-pink flowers in umbels like meadow-sweet, standing up to three foot high. The leaves are actually more like three-sided fleshy spikes, about the thickness of a thin pencil, and seem to be much favoured by dragon-flies in late summer. I once watched one lovely blue fighter-bomber type for a long period alighting on these spikes and boring small holes in them, till some of them looked like old worm-eaten furniture. I assumed it was a lady on a grand egg-laying expedition, but have since read that dragon-flies, if they don't drop their eggs actually in the water, lay them in plant stems some inches beneath the water level. Perhaps this particular dragon-fly was only having a dummy run, getting the hang of the thing before definitely submerging for the real business. Like having a provincial try-out of a play, "prior to West End production."

Orontium aquaticum was our fifth tenant. This was up at the shallow end, like a timid small boy in the school baths. It sends up foot-high stalks with gold-topped white spikes, whence it gets its other and more human name Golden Club.

Lastly, also in the shallows, we had a dwarf Bog Arum, *Calla palustris*, which looked something like a miniature Arum Lily and rather surprised me by producing red berries after flowering.

All the above were planted, not earlier than the end of April, in wire baskets lined with moss and filled with earth. Friar and I then dumped them in the pond in their respective positions and heaped more earth, banked up with stones, round each basket for the roots to spread through. We did this in preference to putting earth over the whole bottom. Our pond being the size it was, by the time we'd spread to the requisite depth there'd hardly have been room for the water. A tip about planting those water-lily roots which have to go in much deeper ponds than ours, is not to put them full fathom five right away, but to stand the baskets on bricks so that they're only about six inches below at first, and then as they send up their new leaves, gradually lower them to the ground floor.

Well, there we were with our first and only pond stocked to capacity—and everything flowered the first summer. A triumph!

Before leaving the subject of ponds, I must record the existence of one of the most delightful of garden catalogues. As I said above, Messrs. Hillier had been favoured with my large and valuable order of six plants-to-go-in-a-pond (aquatics to you, please!), but about the same time I had been given the catalogue of a firm which specialised in supplying everything that a well-dressed pond should have.

It wasn't merely a catalogue either; its full title was "Descriptive Guide to the Garden Pool, Vivarium and Aquarium."[1] It told you practically everything you could want to know, whether you were merely setting up a small indoor aquarium or were going in for a large-sized garden pool. You could be supplied, it seemed, with Peacock-eyed Bass, or Shubunkin goldfish, or Dogfish and Catfish (do they agree in the same pool?) or larvæ of the Great Water Beetle —which is the Nazi of the small pond, for the catalogue says, when stating its food: "Almost any creature weaker than itself." Or you could have Fire-Bellied Toads (at 1s. 6d.) or Mexican Axolotls or Powdered Shrimp (as fish food) or Edible Frogs (as human food—if you felt like it—and off coupon too!) or Green Terrapin—but the list is endless. The Guide also told you how to make your pond in the first place, how to waterproof it, keep it clean and so on. For the sum of 3s. 6d. the firm also stated it would conduct post-mortems on dead fish. If that isn't service I don't know what is.

I confess I was rather tempted to send up a kipper, but felt I didn't know Mr. Haig well enough for that. Or he me.

[1] The firm was L. Haig of Newdigate, Surrey, and the booklet cost 6d.— in 1939.

CHAPTER FIFTEEN

ONE GREAT difficulty about trying to keep a garden going through a long war—like trying to keep anything else going, if it comes to that—is the inability to replace. (I am assuming, of course, that during a war one is lucky enough —as I was, and most humbly thankful too—to be in a position even to *try* and keep it going.) For although any properly-tended garden goes on year after year more or less the same, there are always natural casualties; and very often the victims' places must be filled in the same way, or else some characteristic corner or planned lay-out is spoilt. This, as a rule, can only be done by buying—and during the war invariably what you wanted was "out of stock owing to war conditions."

Take, for instance, our roses. As described in another book, we had at Margarets a rather carefully-planned rose garden. It was primarily a square grass lawn of about 75 foot sides and had a pergola dividing it diagonally down the centre. In either half was one large circular bed and two triangular beds. The circular beds each had twenty-seven bush roses grouped in three varieties, while the triangular beds each had sixteen bushes in four different varieties. Total, if your arithmetic is good, a hundred and eighteen bushes in twenty-two varieties.

Now bush roses don't go on for ever—at least ours never did—and so, to keep up the scheme, occasional replacements were necessary. But when, in 1940, I ordered up the reinforcements as usual, I found I could not get any named variety at all. I tried everywhere, but the most that nurserymen would commit themselves to was "pink," "yellow," "white," or "red." I was faced with upsetting my scheme, or having bare patches in the beds. Determined not to let our garden

be defeated by Hitler, I decided upon bare patches, hoping
to fill them again with the "right people" after the war. To
date, however, early 1946, I have not been able to do so.

Of course the replacement problem was particularly acute
in the flower garden, flowers being presumed to be a luxury

in war. Indeed, judging by the incredible prices charged for
cut flowers in London and other big towns they must have
been for some people not so much a luxury as an unachiev-
able ideal. Here are a few specimen prices asked in 1945 by
leading London florists. Admitted it was winter time, but
it's evident someone was making a lot of money.

Daffodils were 21s. to 25s. per half-dozen, while tulips were in the neighbourhood of 65s. a dozen. Imagine paying 5s. 6d. for a single tulip! Yet carnations were even more, 6s. each, with roses from 7s. 6d. to 10s. apiece. And for an orchid you could pay anything up to a guinea. These florists' profits, it would seem, were a hundred per cent and more, judging by the Covent Garden prices. Chrysanthemums, for instance, selling wholesale in the "Garden" at 1s. to 5s. per bloom, were nowhere less than 3s. 6d. retail, and were often up to 10s. 6d.; lilies at not more than 2s. to 5s. in market were never under 9s. 6d. in any of the bigger shops. And as for violets, 1s. 6d. to 2s. 6d. was being charged for bunches sold at 4d. in Covent Garden. Nice work, if you can get it!

Wholesalers said they didn't like the high prices—I suppose no one cares for the idea of selling something and then seeing it resold at once at double the price—but they blamed the public for paying. On the other hand, in war time flowers for many people, particularly women and town dwellers, cease perhaps to be a luxury which can be done without, but become almost a necessity. When the world is full of evil and strife and ugliness, they are a perpetual reminder of the innocence, peace and beauty that seems to have vanished. (Not all flowers, by the way, are innocent and peaceful. There's a thing, for instance, called a "sundew" which I used eagerly to search for on the Norfolk fens when I was a child. This sweet little bloom, believe it or not, catches and eats flies!)

Vegetables, of course, were in a different class. They were Food, and thus a weapon of war. One recalls how in 1939 the big nurserymen, whose seed catalogues always used to start off with the flower section, suddenly reversed the order. In war flowers had to take a back seat. They were soldiers in scarlet and gold: vegetables were soldiers in khaki battle-dress.[1]

---

[1] Patriotism in this direction can perhaps be overdone. At least this is very definitely the opinion of an elderly couple who had a nice little house in a

There was quite a war-time story, by the way, behind all those neat little packets of vegetable seeds, with the pictures drawn so obviously by the world's most optimistic gluttons, and I remember a long conversation in a railway carriage with a stranger who turned out to be someone high up in Seed Circles. He worked for either Cartier or Carter I think.

He told me something of the importance of the English seed industry in time of war, which of course I had guessed; but he also told me, what I hadn't realised, that in peace a very large percentage of vegetable seed came from abroad— Holland, France, Italy and even North Africa—and one of our great difficulties was replacing this cut-off supply. Personally I should have thought that the U.K. could have grown all the seed required, for neither the product nor the "factories" occupied much space, but he explained that the real trouble was the climate.

Take, for instance, cauliflower seed. I learned that this cannot be grown here at all: the seed-head is just killed by the winter. In normal times most cauliflower seed for this country comes, of all places, from the slopes of Mt. Vesuvius, where whole families of peasants cultivate and gather it specially for the English market. Or, again, take the case of the carrot seed's beard. (A good title that for a detective novel!) Grown in France, the beard falls off naturally in the dry climate. Grown in England, this must be done artificially and expensively.

Incidentally, this carrot seed beard, for the removal of which complicated machinery has had to be evolved, has become quite a profitable by-product. It is highly aromatic —a particularly fascinating and aromatic smell—and is

neighbouring village. During the war the house was lent to an evacuated girls' school while the owner was away. The pride of the garden was a bed of Madonna lilies—established about forty years—which would put up in its due season some two hundred or more stems crowded with bloom. When the owners returned, in the winter of 1945, they found that in an access of "grow-more-food-mindedness" the whole bed had been dug up for vegetables—one small leek still remained as proof—and all the lily bulbs had been just thrown away!

is sold to perfumers. They do not, I gathered, make a perfume of it itself—few women would fall for a scent called *Barbe de Carotte*—but they mix it in with other odours to ginger up morale, as it were.

Again, early broad beans—the Seville for example—are other seeds that must come from abroad; if grown here they lose their early "qualities," and an early bean that is always late is hardly a marketable proposition!

Five years out of seven, I was further told, onion seed cannot be ripened at all in Britain. So with about 98 per cent. of the actual onions we eat in normal times coming from abroad, to grow all one can in war is as much a nationl duty as saving waste paper.

But the actual growing of seed is not the seedsman's only job. Seed heads have to be cut, dried and ripened, and in many cases must be threshed out. Some kinds of seeds—beet is one—are laid on a sheet over a bed of straw and a horsed roller run over them. The seed is thus crushed out, while the "spring" of the straw prevents damage. Small lots of seeds are even flailed.

Then there is the "weeding out," so to speak, of weed-seeds, for by law this has to be done: the Government has laid down a certain standard of purity in the Seeds Act. Also there is the removal of "duds." Among peas, for instance, there will be found split peas, dry rotted peas, and peas with weevil holes. All these have to be removed by every conceivable method from complicated machinery down to girls with good eyesight and quick fingers.

I was quite delighted with the way in which, so my acquaintance told me, the weevil-holed peas were sorted out. The machine is, apparently, a sort of drum, the interior of which is studded with fish-hooks. The seeds are put in, the drum is revolved, and sooner or later every pea with a hole in it has been caught, thus saving the labour of scores of girl sorters. Whether these girls then have to be employed instead on picking the duds off the fish-hooks ready for the next haul I didn't have time to ask, as the train drew in to London and my friend rushed off, leaving me seed-conscious for the rest of my life.

On the whole we at Margarets did not have much difficulty in keeping ourselves supplied with seeds during the war—vegetable seeds, of course, for, as I said, they were part of the country's war effort. And, except for one or two items, we did not save our own seed: we always bought afresh each year and from the old-established firms. It pays in the long run. You can waste almost as much time and labour on seeds, half of which don't come up, as on those which do. Apart from the fact that if you run short of the expected vegetables you have to buy them—and soon lose your cheese-paring profits—whereas it doesn't matter having too much, for someone will be glad of it.

Many, many times during the war were we supremely grateful for our vegetable garden—as a tactical reserve to rations. And a cheap one too: for vegetable prices in London and the big towns were on the high side. Friar used to gasp when I came back and told him what they were asking for cauliflower, lettuce and so on up in the Big Metropolis; for the only prices he knew were those of the weekly Midfield market to which we generally sent any of our surplus. "Cor! And look at the stuff we've got here!" he would comment, and there was quite a new financial gleam in his eye as he ran it over an adjacent cabbage bed. Indeed, he was suddenly all agog to go up to town with a sackful right away— quite forgetting that the price of any given article comprises not only the thing itself, but the fact that is is *where* it is wanted. In other words, our old friend transport.

Onions, however, we did sell in London. Friar had always been very successful in growing them and we used to send up hundredweights and half-hundredweights to my Club, the Savage, or twenty-poundses to favoured friends and trusted onion-lovers in town. In the winter of 1944 we disposed of something over eight hundredweight, and

- MICHAEL D. GIBSON -

171

Friar's only regret was that there was a controlled price. I think he always felt I was lacking in business instinct not to charge more, for I certainly could have got it. But my theory was there were enough people in good old England doing that sort of thing already, and I preferred to be original. However, we did charge for the trouble of sacking them up and for the transport costs, as well as for the sacks—which we sometimes got back.[1]

Whenever I went back to town, too, I always filled a large suitcase with onions, leeks, lettuces and flowers—in short, anything we had to spare—to distribute to friends who were less fortunate. To cut two or three large lettuces, which we at Margarets with so many growing would never have been able to eat, and to hand them over to friends, knowing that they'd have had to pay anything over a shilling per head, was to give one a grand sense of power and lordly munific-ence. One felt like old-time Royalty distributing largesse. "Page! Throw Gaffer Billy Leonard a purse of leeks!" or "Dost look chill, Master Wilfrid Barrett—a paper of onions for thee as a solvent against the rheum!" The liftmen and messengers at the Air Ministry were also most grateful for an occasional haversack of vegetables—much better than a tip!

I used to do the same with eggs too—when our hens were in a generous mood. The quarter-pound tins in which my tobacco came from the Army and Navy Stores were perfect egg-boxes, and just held a couple nicely. Armed with several of these, I used to ask friends to "try my mixture."

Once, I remember, on my way in a taxi to Waterloo en route for a forty-eight at home, I discovered that what I had thought was a tin of tobacco in my pocket was really an overlooked pair of eggs. Evidently I'd made a mistake somewhere during the past week. But what could I do with them? We were approaching the station and it seemed silly to take them back again to the factory after bringing them

[1] Mr. C—— please note.

all the way up—even though no doubt they'd have a grand time boasting about their spree in town to all the other untravelled eggs in the larder.

Then I had a brainwave. I tipped the taxi-driver with them.

I've never seen a more surprised and grateful man. He said: "Well, gov'nor, I've 'ad small tips give me, and big tips give me, and no blinking tips at all give me, but strike me pink, I've never been tipped with *eggs* before."

"*Haven't* you?" I replied in amazement, as though I at least always did it, and sailed into the station to his parting: "They won't 'arf burst theirselves laughing when I tell 'em this on the rank."

In the train I suddenly had *my* laugh. I caught myself wondering just which of my friends' wives next morning would find herself about to tip a quarter-pound of tobacco into the frying-pan—and would ponder for the rest of the day on "that Tony Armstrong's warped sense of humour."

Certainly our hens were real life-savers during the war, but the feeding was a problem. For we had no household scraps: and to suggest that there might be any seemed a reflection on Monica's war-time housekeeping. And anyway Felicity's Tabs came first in the queue for what there was, followed by Sally. Or sometimes preceded by Sally, if she was clever enough to get at the cat plate after wolfing her own dog biscuit and decaying horse-meat ration.[1] The hens, therefore, had to exist on boiled potatoes mashed up with a frightful secret weapon called "balancer meal," which smelt like dead crusader. Maybe it *was* dead crusader. Yet they seemed actually to like the vile concoction. But then they were only hens.

Digressing for a moment, after many years of feeding our hens at week-ends or other times when Friar was not on tap, I've come to the conclusion that these birds are about the

[1] The palmy days of tinned dog foods were of course gone. I'm not certain we didn't have Sally's last tin of "Chappie" ourselves for supper one night in 1942 as a treat.

stupidest creatures God ever made. Even the ant, which has a habit of walking up a six-inch blade of grass and down the other side instead of going an eighth of an inch round, would be considered bright beside the hen in spite of the difference in size of brain.

For what happens when I go to feed the hens? In the first place they cluster round the gate of the run so that you can't get in, and this in spite of the fact that the food is invariably tipped out in a trough at the other end. Any hen that had the sense to wait over there would not only be first at the eats but would have saved its breath by having the food brought to it instead of racing to the gate, and then racing back under my feet as I carry the food to the trough. It would also avoid being painfully trodden on en route, which happens every time to at least three of them.

Then again what happens when one of them gets a big lump, can't swallow it and so retires from the scramble round the trough to tackle it in peace in a corner? All the food is exactly the same, yet about half a dozen others stop eating what they've got and go after this one hen with the big mouthful. They don't get it, because she runs round and round with it; on the other hand she can't eat it because they don't give her time. If she does put it down for a moment and one of the others manages to snatch it, the game of chase is merely resumed, but with a different "he." And this chase may go on for a quarter of an hour till one of them manages to choke the lump back and they return to the trough, to find the remaining hens have cleared up the rest of the food while they've been disputing over one exactly similar mouthful of it.

Or sometimes, as you open the gate and go in, a hen gets out in the excitement. Can it find its way in, though the door out of which it has just come is wide open? No. It will race wildly round the outside of the run, passing the open door each time but flinging itself madly at the wire netting at every other unlikely place, and finally entangling and nearly strangling itself. You have to go out, unwind wire from the gasping, purple-faced idiot, give it first-aid and then lob it over the wire like a grenade.

Other nitwits, who are among the first to greet you at the gate with the bucket of food, follow you excitedly to the trough, snatch a mouthful or so while you are tilting it out in the trough and then leave it, in order to race excitedly after you as you take the empty bucket back. You slam the door in their faces, while they eye the bucket hungrily and are likely to cluster there for hours waiting for food.

Still, I suppose one mustn't blame them. After all, we have the expression "hen-brained" for real stupidity; though personally I now feel it ought not to rank as a mere expression so much as a deadly insult only to be wiped out in blood.

Talking of our hens, I remember one day I was doing the early morning feed and as I'd nearly sprained my ankle by treading on accompanying hens the evening before, I decided I would not let them out of the hen-house till I'd put the food in the trough in peace. I was also anxious to know whether, when I did let them out, they'd make straight for the trough, having heard the usual clanking and scouring of the pail, or whether they'd hang half-wittedly round me till I took them over one by one and pushed their beaks into it.

As a matter of fact neither happened, because of what I can only describe as a charming little domestic incident. The moment I opened the door, a young white hen, whom we called The Blonde, shot out squawking in outraged fashion, hotly pursued by our cockerel who evidently Had Ideas.

Round and round the run they went while all the other hens stood about disapprovingly saying, "Disgraceful!" and, "What he sees in her I can't think," and so on, till at last she happened to flee right across the filled trough of food. The cockerel, in grim pursuit, was halfway across when he saw the food. With what was practically a screaming of brakes, he drew up and in two seconds was scoffing away for dear life, all thoughts of the tender passion driven from his head.

After all, a man must eat. But for the rest of the morning The Blonde stood around in a very obvious sulk.

Still there's one thing I will say for our hens. I do admire them for being able to eat that revolting mess of potato and crusader and turn it into good fresh eggs. Throughout most of the war we had anything from eight to eighteen

birds (including cockerels for eating) and, as I said above, they certainly did us well. Each year too we bought a clutch of eggs and set them under a "broody" and then waited in hopeful expectation, metaphorically fingering our next year's egg-spoons. Rarely of course did more than half the clutch hatch out or survive their moronic parent's heavy-footed tramplings, and even more rarely—for such is nature—did more than a quarter of these turn out to be pullets. But one year, 1944, we achieved what we think is an all-time record for this neighbourhood. We set a clutch of a dozen and hatched out fourteen chicks.

No, there was no deception, no double-yolker twins or anything out of the ordinary run. The explanation is just this: first, a clutch is always a baker's dozen, thirteen; secondly, soon after we set them under the hen she got so tickled with the idea of being a mother that she laid another egg all on her own; and thirdly, quite miraculously, all, fourteen hatched out. And EVEN more miraculously only five of them were cockerels.

CHAPTER SIXTEEN

CHRISTMAS, 1944, found me home on nine days' leave, with the firm conviction that this would be the last "War Christmas," and that my R.A.F. days were now definitely numbered. It turned out, however, that though the final War Christmas, it was not, after all, my last Christmas in uniform; as explained earlier, I eventually stayed on for a few months after the end to finish off my particular job.

I may say here that during the whole of my five years' gruelling service on the Kingsway front I had been lucky enough to get leave every Christmas. Six of them—including the final 1945 one. Of course, when I say that I was *lucky* enough to get leave, I mean it was rather like a story I once heard James Agate tell, of the very popular concert party which visited an R.A.F. Station and gave a show. As there were eight hundred men in the camp and the hall only held two hundred and fifty, the Commanding Officer was asked afterwards by what method the seats had been allocated. "Oh," he said, "we had a ballot for it . . . I was lucky, I got a place in the middle of the front row."

Well, I was somewhat similarly lucky over my Christmas leaves. "Tee Emm" was normally published on the first of each month but I did not follow the usual magazine custom of making the December number the Christmas number. Instead I called our January issue the "Christmas and New Year Number" and brought it out a fortnight ahead of schedule, in mid-December. I did this, of course, solely for the benefit of the Service, so that the boys could have a jolly Yuletide issue nicely in time for Christmas. But funnily enough it also meant that, as the next "Tee Emm" was then not till February, I had a little spare time on my hands round about the end of December. So I was forced to fill it in by going home for Christmas.

Our Christmas at Margarets, as with most homes and families, always followed a certain well-defined routine varied only by the fact that the children were older each year. At my first Service Christmas, for instance, Jomfrey (as you will have gathered from another chapter in this book) was twelve and a half, had not yet left Gresham's Junior School, and was inclined to be still pretty excited about Christmas stockings. By my last one he was seventeen and a half, in the Upper School, Captain of Rugger, and while remaining a staunch supporter of Santa Claus, was no longer a whole-hearted believer in that saint's nocturnal activities. The great Christmas morning "whodunnit" mystery had in fact been solved to his satisfaction.

Of course he kept his knowledge of the big parental fraud from his younger sisters—who in turn politely kept *their* knowledge of it from Monica and myself. Partly, because they felt it gave every one pleasure to pretend: possibly, too, perhaps because they subconsciously realised it was good business, in that it ensured the annual reappearance of those well-filled stockings.

I have often wondered exactly at what age children do discover the Big Secret; and how. It is an interesting field for speculation.

In point of fact, it's a gradual process. The young child begins, naturally, by believing implicitly in the whole business, because as a newcomer to the world his attitude is fundamentally one of complete acceptance. Whether it's his surroundings or himself, or what he is told, or what he invents, it's all equally wonderful and indisputable. To his question, "How does a pumpkin turn into a coach?" your answer, "By magic" is just as good as your answer to "Why does the sun shine?" whether you ascribe it to God or involve yourself in a brief outline of the basic principles of physics and astronomy. Fairyland to a child, in fact, is no more marvellous or inexplicable than the everyday world. As G. K. Chesterton once wrote in his book *Orthodoxy*: "When we are very young children we do not need fairy tales: we only need tales. Mere life is interesting enough."

After a while, as the child grows up, he begins to use his reasoning powers—and a small person can be very logical indeed. A little of childhood's natural acceptance of fairy magic as a definite component of real life has vanished. He is inclined to say, like the man from Missouri, "you gotta *show* me." After he has persistently tried to see fairies and has failed, has even failed to find any convincing trace of their activities beyond the occasional dance-ring, he begins to be a little sceptical. There's no real evidence. No old woman is transformed in front of his eyes in order to give him three wishes: no white swan asks him to be released from a spell; he never gets even the briefest of glimpses of a Grand Ten-Round Prince *versus* Dragon Contest; and when he asks to be directed to the nearest witch or giant he is probably laughed at. But shaken though his faith in all this other world of the fairy books may be, he is not going to doubt the existence of Santa Claus for a while yet, because—well, seeing's believing. A stocking empty overnight *is* definitely bulging with toys next morning. Evidence enough even for a fairly young Missourian. Must be *something* in it.

Later on, as his ability to reason develops still further, he at last begins to suspect something a little phoney. How, for instance, do the reindeer balance on the steeply sloping roof? Or how does Santa Claus get round to every one in the one night—especially as he has seen the old gentleman only that afternoon up to his eyes in work at Selfridge's. And then this business about the chimney; his bedroom one is pretty small for an old fellow of Father Christmas' build. Sometimes, of course, this last is countered by his parents suggesting the window as an alternative to the chimney—rather like some erudite antiquarian scholar producing an emendation to an accepted translation of an old manuscript; "Professor Gutz has evidently overlooked the fact that the

original Sanscrit word is capable of two different inter-
pretations."

To what extent, by the way, the synthetic Santa Claus' of
Selfridge's and elsewhere are believed in is a moot point. I
still have a letter of Christmas, 1943, from Felicity to the
gentleman who was that year taking the part of Santa Claus
at a large shop in Midfield. He had apparently been asking
visiting children to write their requests to him—evidently
hoping they would be intercepted by parents, as Felicity's
was. Her letter went:

"Dear Father Christmas, I would very much like to
have some Embroydery silks to sow with, as I have just
made a bag for mother, and I want to make it pretty. I
am eight, I am that little girl with fair hair and plaits
which came to visit you on the Friday about a fortnight
ago.

"Love, Felicity."

How genuine that is, I don't know. It was discovered,
sealed down, and waiting for post, on the hall table. It rings
true enough—and after all, she had taken the trouble to
provide Father Christmas with explicit identifying details
as to who it was writing to him! On the other hand, Monica
thinks that the child knew well enough what she was doing,
and that like war-time fake messages in an already broken
cipher, it was intended to be not only intercepted, but acted
upon.

Still, I once watched children queuing up in one big
London store to receive a present (already surreptitiously
paid for by the attendant grown-ups) from the hands of
Santa himself; and unshakeable belief was writ large on
many a small face. Reminding me of the story of the kid
who returned to his parents and said: "I know now it's
really Father Christmas, mummie; when I went up behind
him to look in the bran-tub, he turned round and acksherly

spoke to me." "What did he say, darling?" He said: "Hop it, you little bastard, and get in the queue with the others.'"

Probably the answer to the question is that the children don't believe really that the figure in red dressing-gown and white beard is actually Santa Claus. Obviously it is someone

impersonating him, *but* it doesn't make the original any less real. No sharp-eyed youngster at a party with his: "That's not Father Christmas, that's only uncle," has really shattered any faith, even his own, at one fell blow—any more than the appearance in a play of an understudy means that the star does not really exist. The explanation is so simple: Santa himself was busy, and kind uncle was helping out.

As a rule I think the whole game is generally given away —or rather the first *real* seeds of suspicion are sown—by other children. The patronising elder brother thinks it's time the youngsters knew about it. Or the small boy is mocked by that horrible little girl who taunts: "Hoo! You *don't* believe in Santa Claus, *do* you? Soppy thing!" Or else an older and more experienced man-about-nursery takes an innocent behind the woodshed and, by way of showing off, confides to him the awful Facts of Christmas Life.

All this then leads to watching at night and possibly a parent being caught red-handed—though in general the child has little chance of this. However determinedly he keeps awake "actually to *see* Father Christmas," the parents are equally determined on waiting till he has gone to sleep— and the odds are that they're in better training for late hours than he is.

Often, too, the question, "Is Santa Claus *real*?" is broached direct, which leads to a tricky tussle between parental consciences and a desire to keep up the traditional belief as long as possible.

But the great thing is that, even when the child has found out, he invariably decides in his mind to ignore the discovery. For he is not so very old after all—and even though fairies and magic can be proved not to exist, there's always "Let's pretend."

How long Old Man Santa remains thus, as a welcome but debunked annual visitor, I wouldn't know. As I said, the tradition is still rampant in our family. But I heard just a few days ago of an only daughter of twenty-eight, living with her parents, who still gets, and gives in return, a Christmas stocking; still, too, as a Top Secret operation. At least she and her mother give each other one. The father, wise man, takes no active part. He told me, however, that each year he hears them at dead of night, as he put it, "dodging each other in the passage and catching their deaths of pneumonia."

Our children, as I said above, still hang their stockings up—and Monica and I have under pressure to hang up ours. Five of them in a row on our bedroom mantelpiece, varying in size from Felicity's small one to Toni, who this last Christmas hung up a school gym stocking about fifteen feet long and capable of stretching to the proportions of a bolster. (She found it next day with only the top third in service, a string having been tied tightly round at that point with a label "Rationed.") My own stocking generally turns out to be the clown dog of the troupe—the ultimate target for all practical joking. I've learned to put my hand in pretty gingerly next morning. One year it was gorse and holly: next year it may well be cold porridge. What I'm really scared of is that it'll be a lightly-set mousetrap.

The Really Important Thing, however, in our Christmas at Margarets is our equivalent of " getting in the Yule Log." That is to say, digging up the Christmas Tree. It's almost a tradition with us now.

When first the house was built we used always at Christmas time to buy from the local nurseryman a small fir-tree —generally the top end of a slightly larger fir-tree. It was furtively installed in the drawing-room on Christmas Eve and by next day had borne fruit, which was duly pillaged after lunch. Then, like the tree in Hans Andersen's fairy-story, it sat around in its dignity for a few days, covered with coloured lights and "snow" and three or four overlooked half-melted chocolates, and finally after its crowded hour of glorious life, was relegated to outer darkness, till such time as it could be burnt without the children seeing the sacrilege.

A couple of years before the war, however, we suddenly discovered we had been given for once a real small fir-tree, with actually a few roots on it. So after its tour of duty we planted it out in a corner of the garden on the offchance —and it actually throve.

So next year we had it up again and repeated the performance. And so we have done ever since. In gratitude for the reprieve it makes a little growth every year, thus keeping about level with Jomfrey's growth. He, at any rate, has had no reason to wonder "*why* do Christmas trees get smaller every Christmas?" which is generally one of the first distressing intimations that you are getting older. (Another occurs somewhere about the forties, when it suddenly dawns on you how *young* all the policemen are!)

On the tree go a large assortment of presents—including something for Friar and Mrs. Friar, who invariably attend the harvesting ceremony on Christmas afternoon and Take Wine with us. Friar's present is easy: it's generally something in an Envelope and something in a Bottle.

Other presents, however, are always a problem—owing to war scarcities; usually we end up weakly with book-tokens. Felicity one year took the thing up in a most business-like way by making out in advance a list of what she wanted. I still have it, and it's pretty comprehensive—some two dozen items. They range from "Postalauder" (amount left to donor's generosity) down to "Orange" and "Sugar Lump"—obviously intended to be in partnership. Two items surprised us: one was "Lover's Calendar," for which we felt she was surely a little young yet; and the other was quite simply "Horse." ("Something in the Arab style, moddam? Or would you prefer a Percheron?") We discovered, however, that the absence of a hyphen and the incidence of the end of a line had turned into two demands what should have been one, "Horse-Lover's Calendar."

She didn't go slow on the publicity angle of the business either. For days before Christmas she was busy making copies of the list. Every one who was in the house or who even came into it was given one, while about every other minute, it seemed, one was asked, "Have you got a copy of my list? I've got one here if you haven't." She should really have borrowed a Roneograph for the job. Copies were also distributed, like hand-bills, all over the place—every good advertising site, mantelpieces, doors, picture-frames, even the lavatory seat, being pre-empted very early on. The general effect was like the aftermath of a leaflet raid over Germany.

But this is all getting very personal, and so on this scene of one family's season of Peace and Goodwill it seems a good idea to draw the curtain of the whole play. For, except for a final small chapter, I seem to have reached—or rather wandered through to—the end of the book.

CHAPTER THE LAST

THE WAR had ended. The finish had come with slight warning in the case of Germany, the arch-enemy; but with hardly any in the case of the little Eastern sub-humans. With surprising abruptness the nightmare which had dominated the world for six years had ceased to be. Six years of such bitter hatred, grinding effort, cruelty, heroism, broken faith, disruption of sane and ordered life, self-sacrifice and misery as the world can never before have known. Hundreds of thousands had been killed or maimed or broken in health while fighting their fellow-men. Hundreds of thousands more, innocent civilians, had also perished. Worst crime of all, perhaps, six million of the Jewish race alone had fallen victims to the German *Herren-volk's* insane and sadistic policy of deliberate extermination for no better reason than the faith they held, and many thousands of these had perished *before ever* the nations went to war.

Then, all of a sudden, it was at an end. It happened so swiftly that one could hardly grasp it. The sense of relief and thankfulness was temporarily swamped by the realisation that the whole framework of life as one had known it for the better part of a decade, had abruptly vanished. One faced an unknown existence in which only one thing was certain; that though the blood and tears had gone, the toil and sweat remained, that the grim aftermath was yet to come. And like a black cloud the shadow of the first atomic bombs hung fearfully over the world's conscience. Humanity stood at the cross-roads.

Still, it was over.

And at least that fact could be celebrated. Pent-up emotions were released like a coiled spring. After the curtain-raiser of VE Day, the real thing, VJ Day, had arrived.

London—in the wake of New York which as usual had celebrated two or three false alarms—went mad. Presumably every other place did too. Even on VE Day East Downing had had its own personal triumphal bonfire, largely—and naturally—of black-out material, a main part of the structure being our contribution from Margarets of two large basket-chairs from the garden.

I watched, and was one of, the large crowd in Trafalgar Square that sunny VJ afternoon, which had collected for no other reason than the fun of just collecting. A police band was there and was playing to the crowd, and in particular there was a girl whom many must remember, for on the curved parapet of the eastern basin, she danced for over an hour her interpretation of the broadcast music for our entertainment. Occasionally she fell in the water. Either she was destined to go on the stage, or was determined to get on the stage, or was already on the stage, for she certainly held her audience—an audience, too, to delight any young girl's heart. For part of the time an airman and a soldier danced on either side of her. Occasionally they too fell in. Finally she and several other girls and soldiers waded out to the central fountain, climbed up into the bowl and went on dancing there. A few minutes later the rival western basin crowd, which was neither so talented or ingenious as we were, followed suit.

At intervals the music stopped and the Voice of Authority pleaded that no more people should climb up into the fountains, which strangely enough had not been designed as dance floors, but merely to hold a small amount of water —"we don't want accidents on a day like this, do we?" Nobody paid the slightest attention, and I don't think Authority really cared. After all, had they been in earnest, they could always have turned the fountains on. . . .

At four-thirty—with a friend, Nigel Deare, just released from the Navy and who was acting as my Transport Officer and staying the night—I left for the country. . . .

I wandered round my garden at dusk and was deeply and truly grateful that unlike so many, many homes and families in the world, mine had been spared. . . .

I'm afraid this book has been a terrible mixture—bits about the garden, London, war, quite unforgivable stories about the children, not much about the house, and far too many digressions about nothing in particular. Still, it has had to be written in odd moments over a period of five years —and after all when you're only exercising remote control, you're not very certain exactly what *is* going on at the remote distance.

Looking back, too, on this record of small things done in the house and garden, of small family incidents, it may all seem rather parochial in a world just emerged from one of the greatest struggles of history. It looks as though, because I had had one war at close range in my life, I had kept well out of range in this. It perhaps gives the impression that I had merely been concerned with little troubles and joys at Margarets, while democracy's very existence was at stake.

But then the book is only intended to be about the small incidents in one small English home, and is not about big issues like the survival of democratic principles in the world.

Or—I wonder—is it? For what *exactly* is democracy? As Joad would put it, it all depends on what you mean by democracy.

Well, democracy is, at its simplest or dictionary level, a form of government by the people or through officers appointed by them. It is government "of the people, by the people, for the people." It is the antithesis of rule by one tyrant or one dominant party for personal ends. And it is with this latter type of rule in its worst and filthiest form that democracy has been grappling to the death for so long. Thus for nearly six years the word "democracy" has been a trumpet call: it has been a flaming symbol in the sky, a Holy Grail, an ideal for which to lay down one's life. It has been raised to the status of "absolutes" like Truth and Justice, for which down the years men have also fought and died.

But *is* democracy an "absolute," an imponderable "truth" which all men at once recognise in their hearts? If so, then why did not that great democratic nation, the U.S.A. across the seas, take up arms the moment the world's *democratic* way of life was threatened? Because they were unprepared for war? Admitted. But, after all, they were, at the time of Munich, pretty liberal—to say the least of it—with criticisms of Britian, also then totally unprepared, for not fighting on behalf of democracy in the shape of Czecho-Slovakia.

Later we did go to war in the cause of freedom—still sadly unprepared, *but* of our own volition. And within nine months we were alone—a fact that with the usual British penchant for blowing every other national trumpet but their own one may well be forgotten sooner than it should. But a further eighteen months were still to elapse before the U.S.A. took up arms in the same cause, democracy, and even then not entirely of her own volition but because Japan had attacked her. Was, therefore, America truly fighting for an immediately recognisable "absolute" called democracy, or for something else. And what was our other great ally, Russia, also brought in by being attacked, fighting for too? Surely not for "democracy"—for by no stretch of imagination can that great and amazing nation be said to have a truly democratic government as we know it. No, both were fighting *simply and solely because they were attacked and their Way of Life was threatened.*

For democracy is *not* the "absolute" it has appeared to be in these last years. Democracy is simply the right to live one's own individual life without interference from the State—or at least without any more interference from the State than is necessary to protect the freedom of other individuals in the State. Democracy protects the individual's

Way of Life within the state, whereas Totalitarianism absorbs the individual into the State. This has been well expressed (by, I think Wickham Steed in a Sunday paper—though I may be giving a wrong credit): "The State is a means, not an end. . . . It should be valued in terms of the service it can render to an individual."

And if this is so, what is more individual than one's home and family and garden, the frame-work of one's own small life, such as I have written about in these pages. I do *not* think these matters are parochial and that therefore they should not be considered when big causes like democracy are being fought for and men and women are dying for them. For these people are *not* fighting and dying for an ideal, so much as their *conception of an ideal*—and that ideal is just to live freely and happily with their families in their own homes. It was for this, for instance—the safety of their homes and villages and streets and fields—that a million Home Guards came into existence overnight. They were prepared to fight not for the ideal itself, but for what the ideal represented immediately to them.

And so, ending—like every four films out of five during 1943 and 1944—with the central character coming forward to the camera and loosing off That Speech about Demarcracy —I make no apology for having written this book about my little corner of England, and what was just *our* Way of Life then at Margarets.

THE END